The success factor

All that is gold does not glitter,
Not all those who wander are lost;
The old that is strong does not wither,
Deep roots are not reached by the frost.
From the ashes a fire shall be woken,
A light from the shadows shall spring;
Renewed shall be blade that was broken,
The crownless again shall be king.

J. R. R. Tolkien[1]

The
success
factor
Denis Haack

INTER-VARSITY PRESS

INTER-VARSITY PRESS
38 De Montfort Street, Leicester LE1 7GP, England

© Denis Haack 1989

All rights reserved. No part of this publication may be reproduced, stored in a retrieval system, or transmitted, in any form or by any means, electronic, mechanical, photocopying, recording or otherwise, without the prior permission of Inter-Varsity Press.

Unless otherwise stated, Scripture quotations in this publication are from the Holy Bible, New International Version. Copyright © 1973, 1978, 1984 International Bible Society. Published by Hodder & Stoughton Ltd.

First published in the United States of America under the title
The Rest of Success

First British edition 1989

British Library Cataloguing in Publication Data
Haack, Denis, 1947 –
[The rest of success] The success factor.
1. Personal failure. Personal success.
Christian viewpoints
I. Title
248.4

ISBN 0-85110-849-0

Typeset in the United States of America

Printed in Great Britain by Cox and Wyman Ltd, Reading

Inter-Varsity Press is the book-publishing division of the Universities and Colleges Christian Fellowship (formerly the Inter-Varsity Fellowship), a student movement linking Christian Unions in universities and colleges throughout the United Kingdom and the Republic of Ireland, and a member movement of the International Fellowship of Evangelical Students.
For information about local and national activities write to UCCF, 38 De Montfort Street, Leicester LE1 7GP.

For Margie Lou

Chapter 1: Something Everyone Wants	11
Chapter 2: Christian Views of Success	25
Chapter 3: The World's Measure of Success	37
Chapter 4: Where Success and Idolatry Meet	51
Chapter 5: Case Studies in the Failure of Success	65
Chapter 6: How God Uses the World's Success	87
Chapter 7: Seeing Our Work the Way God Does	109
Chapter 8: Faithfulness in Some Trouble Spots	133
Chapter 9: What the World Didn't Tell You about Motivation	155
Notes	177

Acknowledgments

I want to acknowledge some friends who were willing to give precious time and energy to read various parts and versions of this book with red pen in hand. They sharpened my thinking, encouraged me to continue and helped delete a lot of clutter.

To Steve Garber, Butch and Mary Williams, Jean Baue, Barbara Kinnick, Greg and Mary Jane Grooms, Carl Esbeck, Dr. Herbert Schlossberg, Sarah Peeples, Lendol Calder, Bill Moeny and Marylu Warwick I give my thanks.

To my wife, Margie, who gave ideas, the freedom to spend extra hours bent over the word processor, much encouragement and many hours of typing—my appreciation for your willingness to see this through to completion.

Andy Le Peau, Stephen Board, Rodney Clapp and LaVonne Neff gave valuable help during the editing process.

I trust you can all see your suggestions in these pages. The folly that remains, of course, is my own.

Lastly, I want to acknowledge all of you who were unstinting in prayer as I slogged through various drafts of this book. Unfortunately, there are too many of you to mention here. I suspect that neither you nor I will recognize the extent of your role until we are together in heaven.

The Three Basic Tenets of Successful Failureship

Tenet #1: Be Positive You Are Going to Fail
(Try to the utmost of your ability but always expect to fail)

Tenet #2: Make Each Failure a Success
(Since you expected to fail, when you do fail you have succeeded—at failing)

Tenet #3: Make Each Success a Failure
(If you do happen to succeed, then you have failed since you should have been expecting failure.
But since failure was your goal and you failed because you succeeded, you have succeeded—in failing)
The Journal of Irreproducible Results

More than any other time in history, mankind faces a crossroads. One path leads to despair and utter hopelessness. The other, to total extinction. Let us pray we have the wisdom to choose correctly.
Woody Allen

CHAPTER 1

SOMETHING EVERYONE WANTS

There were fourteen seconds left in the final game of the basketball tournament. We were behind by one point. Jim brought the ball down the court and glanced at the clock. Ten seconds. The plan was to get the ball to Stan, our best player, but he was too closely guarded to get a shot off. The ball went from Jim to Stan and back to Jim again. Five seconds. Four. He passed to me. Three. Two. I shot. As the buzzer sounded, the ball seemed to hang in the air before swishing through the net. The roar in the gym was deafening. We had won!

Have you ever had that sort of daydream? I have, repeatedly. The thrill of making that final crucial shot must be wonderful.

I wouldn't know; I never made the team.

The Sweet Taste of Success

Most of us prefer success to failure—even in our fantasies. We define success and failure differently, but however we define them, they help to shape our thinking and our lives. Regardless of how competitive we are, succeeding is important to all of us.

One of my warmest memories from school involved a race between my best friend and me for the top mark in trigonometry. It had long before been determined that Martin and I would both get *A*'s. All that remained in the contest was to see which of us could accumulate the most points in the process.

We relished being an elite company of two. It didn't bother us when our classmates grumbled about it. Both Martin and I had endured eleven years of always being chosen last for teams in Physical Education. We thought it was only justice to have our chance in first place. Besides, the athletes received jackets; we academics just got pins from the National Honor Society—pins no one ever wore. So we didn't feel too bad about enjoying a rare moment at the top.

I have no idea why the competition occurred in maths; Martin and I were in several classes together. Neither of us was interested in trig, and I can't say I ever grasped the value of cosines for everyday life. Nevertheless, by the middle of the term the competition was in full swing. Mr. Thompson, our teacher, put the updated point totals on the notice-board each Monday, and that helped keep the race alive.

Late in the year Mr. Thompson surprised us with a test the day after setting us a new topic for study. Rather than having studied, Martin and I had gone to a basketball game. So we blundered our way through the test, being careful, of course, to put our names on the paper. That was always worth one point. We weren't very bothered about being unprepared. We each felt secure in the knowledge that the other was equally in the dark, and the rest of the class was too far behind to even count.

The following day our papers were returned. Mr. Thompson had a peculiar way of performing this task. He would arrange the marked papers in order so he could move slowly down the rows of seats. He would first glance at our mark and then, looking us squarely in the eye, place our paper face down before us.

He came to me first. I quickly lifted the corner of my paper to catch a glimpse of the mark: *D*. I left it face down. Martin received his paper next, and for some incomprehensible reason, turned it face up. He had an *F*. You can imagine what I did. With great flourish and pride, I turned my paper over for him to see. I was elated. I had beaten him. No *D* ever looked so magnificent!

There was, of course, no reason for me to feel good about my mark—my father certainly wouldn't have been impressed. I hadn't done the assigned work, didn't know the required material, and the *D* on the test proved it. Still, I felt wonderful. I had a feeling of accomplishment, even though my performance represented failure. I had received the second poorest mark in the class, but felt like a winner.

I remember very little from that school trigonometry class. I don't recall the formulas we used, and I couldn't tell you the difference between a sine and a cosine. What I do remember is how important it was to succeed.

Savoring Failure

The contest in trigonometry was a minor affair, but it seemed important to me at the time. Every part of our life has some notion of success and failure associated with it which colors our priorities, our goals and our self-image. Whether or not we think much about it, succeeding is important to us.

If you doubt the importance of succeeding, consider failing. Not "I've failed in this one little thing," or, "This isn't quite up to my normal brilliant standards," but *"I'm a failure."* A failure, not in the narrow sense of dropping a ball, but of being washed up as a player.

I felt that way the summer our two-year-old daughter Marsena fell from the second story of a house. I was directing a one-week church camp, and my family was staying in an old adobe house that stood on a hill. Half of the second floor of the two-story structure was a large open-air balcony that jutted out over the edge of the hill. A three-foot fence enclosed this flat roof area. I remember checking it out and deciding it was child-proof, as long as we kept Marsena from climbing the fence. I told my wife Margie I thought it would be a good place for her and Marsena to spend time together. They enjoyed that balcony, especially in the mornings and at dusk, when the New Mexico air was clear and mild.

It happened in a moment. Marsena had been playing when she suddenly tripped, fell and rolled out under the fence. When we reached her, she was lying on her back on the rocks below the house, bleeding and in shock. Carefully gathering her up in our arms, we raced the twenty-plus miles into the nearest town. The tiny clinic there didn't have a dependable x-ray machine, so we had to retrace our steps and then drive on to Albuquerque.

I don't think Margie and I have ever experienced such a flood of emotion as during those next awful hours. Mixed in with the fear and horror was a deep sense of failure. Marsena wasn't to blame for what had happened. It was our responsibility as parents to make sure things were safe. Why hadn't I looked more closely at that fence? Why had I assumed the only danger was going *over* it? Margie and I reassured each other that we weren't blaming the other for the tragedy that had interrupted our lives. But even that didn't erase the nagging conviction that we had failed. Because of that failure, our little girl might have died.

Become deeply convinced you're a failure, and a profound darkness descends. Such a self-image colors all of life: every plan, every judgment, every relationship, every dream. A young woman, wrestling with an overwhelming sense of failure and meaninglessness, described it this way:

> It was a black cloud of depression. It envelops you. You cannot get out. You don't think life will ever get better. You can't conceive of it. You can't imagine it. You can't even dream it. And you're going to die anyway: life's this long corridor with all of these doors, and death is the last one, so why not now? It's so painful to live that it seems less painful to die.[1]

For some this isn't abstract theory—it's their honest perception of reality. And more than a few, like this teen-ager, have sacrificed their lives in their despair. The tragedy of suicide should be enough to convince us of the importance of success and failure in people's lives and thinking.

Fortunately, for most of us the struggle with failure is less extreme. Although we may occasionally refer to ourselves as "a total failure," we usually don't mean it in this absolute sense. Every failure can feel—at least momentarily—like the end of the world, in spite of what we know to be objectively true. "I'm so embarrassed I could just die," we say.

I wrote a book review a few years ago which I had intended to be thought-provoking. Instead it turned out to be primarily negative. I'd wanted to raise some questions, but hadn't intended to be as down on the book as the review ended up sounding. It was hard to write a letter of apology, and the experience nearly convinced me I should never again try to publish my work.

Our failures seem worse because some individuals appear to sail effortlessly from one accomplishment to another throughout their lives. They achieve more than the rest of us have strength to dream about. Hearing them say we just can't see their failures is small consolation.

For most of us, life is a mixed bag. Few of us get to the top (wherever that is), but few of us scrape bottom either. Our ups and downs seem to largely balance out—or at least remain manageable—as we concentrate on our successes and rationalize our failures.

Few consciously aim to fail. But life is complicated by forces beyond our control that can interrupt and overturn what we were working so hard to achieve. The outcome of our efforts doesn't depend on us alone. Even with our best efforts, failure can raise its ugly head. And our fear of it shows just how important succeeding is to us.

The Significance of Succeeding

Our failures are made worse if we have doubts about the value of our successes. Sometimes coping consists of little more than plunging resolutely ahead. The fear is that if we slow down and take a hard look at things, our successes may amount to little more than insignificant blips in the blueprint of history.

Our definition of success and failure tells a great deal about what we hold most dear. What we treasure, Jesus taught, reveals where our heart is (Mt 6:21). At the very least, we want to feel that we count for something, that our achievements are valuable. The sense of a job well done is deeply satisfying. This sense of meaning and accomplishment is basic to the enchantment of success.

Success devoid of meaning is simply failure by another name. Nobody wants that. An easy way to deflate a person's moment in the spotlight is to suggest that, yes, you succeeded, but so what? Why strive so hard for such a big nothing?

The link between our definitions of significance and success is a key to why some things are not important to us. I read recently of a man who has one of the best collections of bricks in the world. Some of them have been dated to hundreds of years before Christ. There was no doubt about it; he was very proud of his bricks. He was clearly a success at brick collecting. His biggest problem, he said, was the cost and effort required to transport them to brick-collector conventions. My reaction was disbelief. Bricks? Who would want to collect bricks or attend brick conventions?

But there's more to this connection between success and meaning. If success continually eludes us, we can begin to feel somehow less real, less substantial, less meaningful. It's impossible for human beings to live as though there's no meaning in life. We want success because it seems to reassure us of our significance.

This yearning for significance is built into the fabric of our humanness.[2] We weren't created for meaninglessness. Creatures made in God's image know implicitly that life is more than mere chance or chaos (Rom 1:19-20).

The Rat Race
In today's world the importance of succeeding has taken on

added weight. Cut loose from its religious and philosophical moorings, Western culture has rejected belief in absolute truth.[3] The resulting relativism has sucked significance from life. Still, people speak of and desire success. For many, cultural success is the only remaining standard for a meaningful life.

For some that means making it to the top of their field. Or achieving such wealth or expertise that the rest of the world stops and takes notice. But few manage to get to the top. Some of us aren't even in jobs that have a top to strive for. The biggest crowd is always at the bottom, looking up.

But relativism has done more than this. It has worked magic on success itself. Today there need be no real work, no real accomplishment, no real achievement involved. The new success is open to everyone. "Indeed it has no reference to anything outside the self," writes Christopher Lasch. "The new ideal of success has no content."[4] All you have to do is *look* successful—and you *are*. Thus we have the great emphasis on appearances and endless strategies to succeed at success.

The popularity of this subject is reflected by the number of books published on success. Some are how-to books, and the advice extends to the kind of underwear to purchase. When you have a shower at the leisure centre, you want people to see you're "designer-label" all the way down! Most of these publications attempt to be motivational—though manipulative is sometimes closer to the truth. A few are little more than crass encouragement to get all you can, no matter how barbarous the process or how deadly the result. In spite of some helpful ideas in some of these books, many are merely drivel.

Much of this material on success is a rehash of the same ideas dressed up with a new twist or two. It boils down to a type of pop psychology: live for yourself, be optimistic, make plans, be more assertive, look the part, and with a bit of luck and hard work you can get your share of the pie. The fact that they sell so well tells us something of the hunger for significance and meaning so many feel in their lives.

All this interest in success points up how important succeeding is to us. Even if we're not compulsive about it, most of us probably prefer success to failure—however we define it.

Varieties of Success

There can be almost as many variations on success and failure as there are people. One person may put down another's perspective on success as silly, or ridiculous, or even evil. One person's success may look like failure to another, but that doesn't alter the driving force behind each one's standard.

The film *The Breakfast Club* showed a highly disparate group of school students in detention together. Each one had a vision of what it meant to succeed and to fail. The Cheerleader had little in common with either the Dirtball or the Brain, but each of them had goals and values—and each struggled to achieve them.[5]

Peer pressure can be an important element in defining success. We're all affected by the notions of success held by those around us. Sometimes we even adopt standards we heartily dislike. Referring to the 1980s, one commentator has remarked,

> The pressure to excel is greater than it has ever been, but being successful in the eyes of others isn't really what a lot of people would choose for themselves. Still, they feel that they must pursue that goal even if it means crawling over the bodies of co-workers or sacrificing what they really want.[6]

Whole communities or classes of people adopt notions of success and failure. In the 1950s, people worked and saved in order to get a house, a TV, a car, and a better education for their children. Those things became symbols of success and soon were considered normative. During this period I lived in the Orient. The rural peasants there set their sights on something very different. Although small in Western eyes, their symbol of success was as important to them as the more affluent Western items were to us. They worked and saved to own a cigarette lighter. This was their measure of success.

The symbols of success can include smart suits or faded blue jeans, big luxury cars or small energy-conscious ones, debt or lack of personal debt, deep faith or skepticism, involvement with Amnesty International or membership of a shooting club. That many of these are of doubtful significance does little to alter their value as measures or symbols of success.

People the world over order their lives around a definition of ultimate success and failure. Soviet bureaucrats maneuvering up the Party apparatus, Hindus washing in the filthy Ganges River, and Yuppies elbowing their way up the career structure appear, on the surface, to have little in common. Yet aren't they all pursuing what they see as the path to success?

Wherever we look, we see evidence of the importance of success in people's lives. Succeeding, or at least avoiding failure, drives their existence.

This is true for Christians as well. Whether we know it or not, a concept of success is part of our world view. We each have a working definition of failure and a desire to keep from its clutches. With so much pressure to succeed, we need to be aware of what our notion of success is, what its roots are, and what the implications are for our lives. We must be sure our perspective on success and failure is in accord with the truth of God's Word.

To do this requires two things. First, we must critique the definitions of success that we find around us. They must be analyzed to see if they are true or if they dishonor our Lord. Then we can turn to the task of developing a uniquely Christian alternative, a robustly biblical model of success. These two steps form the basic outline I've followed in this book.

Competing visions of success come at us from religious and secular sources. In chapter two I examine the definitions of success taught in Christian circles, and in chapter three look at the definitions given by modern society. Unfortunately, they're all insufficient. The central danger with these erroneous views of success is that they can open us to idolatry, which is the topic of chapter four.

In the second half of the book I seek to develop the beginnings of a biblical model of success. In chapter five we'll take a look at a series of character studies from the Bible. In each case the goal will be to discern what was central to their failure or success before God. In chapter six I explore the ways in which God can use societal success and failure in people's lives. We'll be attempting to answer the question, How do the world's standards of success mesh with biblical standards? Then, in chapter seven I look at what it means to follow our Lord in our work while chapter eight examines the rest of life. Finally, in chapter nine I answer the question of what should motivate us until our King returns.

So, let's begin. We'll start by looking at the popular versions of success found in Christian circles. That's the subject of the next chapter.

Questions for Individuals and Groups

1. What experiences from childhood were important for your understanding of success and failure?

2. How did your parents define success and failure? How has that affected your perspective? In what ways, if any, have your views diverged from theirs? Why? How has this affected your relationship with them or their view of you?

3. What definition of success and failure seems to be normative in your work? your neighborhood? In what ways do you agree or disagree?

4. What type of failure do you most fear? Why?

5. In what areas of life do you find success easy? difficult? Why do you think this is? What pressures do you face which keep you from succeeding as you'd like? What should you do?

6. Have you ever chosen to fail when you could have succeeded? Would you do the same again?

7. What is your greatest success as a Christian? your greatest failure?

Fame is like a river, that beareth up things light and swollen,
and drowns things weighty and solid.
Francis Bacon

How is it possible for the man who designed Voyager 19,
which arrived at Titania, a satellite of Uranus, three seconds off
schedule and a hundred yards off course after a flight
of six years, to be one of the most screwed-up creatures in
California—or the Cosmos?
Walker Percy

Prosperity Theology is especially devious in its ability
to lead a person out on a limb of truth, and then let him cut
himself off with the saw of his own imagination. The tragedy, of
course, is that on his way down the individual is usually foolish
enough to fund the rascal who put him there in the first place!
Doug Sherman and William Hendricks

CHAPTER 2

CHRISTIAN VIEWS OF SUCCESS

As important as it is to have a Christian view of success, we're immediately faced with a dilemma. Our problem comes from the diversity of teaching on success in Christian circles. There are competing definitions, and each one claims to be scriptural. If you don't have your wits about you, it can become very confusing. By and large, these Christian versions of success come in three varieties: the Gospel of Prosperity, the Gospel of Simple Living, and Success by Default.

Success for the Children of the King
The Gospel of Prosperity, appearing in many guises, begins with the observation that the Bible specifically mentions success. And the Bible is quite positive about it! The interpretation is obvious

to anyone who can read: The Lord wants you to succeed.

> Be strong and very courageous. Be careful to obey all the law my servant Moses gave you; do not turn from it to the right or to the left, *that you may be successful* wherever you go. Do not let this Book of the Law depart from your mouth; meditate on it day and night, so that you may be careful to do everything written in it. *Then you will be prosperous and successful.* (Josh 1:7-8, emphasis mine)

> Dear friend, I pray that you may enjoy good health and *that all may go well with you,* even as your soul is getting along well. (3 Jn 2, emphasis mine)

> Blessed is the man who does not walk in the counsel of the wicked or stand in the way of sinners or sit in the seat of mockers. But his delight is in the law of the LORD, and on his law he meditates day and night. He is like a tree planted by streams of water, which yields its fruit in season and whose leaf does not wither. *Whatever he does prospers.* (Ps 1:1-3, emphasis mine)

One time I heard a TV preacher declare, as he pointed to his diamond rings and new Cadillac, that the difference between him and us was that "I have Cadillac faith and you have Volkswagen faith." He exhorted us to increase our faith and suggested that only a "liberal view" of the Scriptures could derive any other interpretation than the one that was obvious to him. By the end of his message I was led to believe that to own anything less than the most expensive was not only an indication of anemic faith, but a slap at the dignity and generosity of the God of Abraham. And Abraham happened to be, by the way, a very wealthy man.

Often there are prerequisites to receiving God's prosperity. Some say prayer is the secret. Others suggest we must claim

God's promises, and still others recommend Bible memorization. In each case the teaching is similar: God's will for us is to be prosperous—just reread those verses!—and if we would just believe, or claim, or memorize, then success would flow from the windows of heaven. If we aren't successful, the fault lies with us: we are unbelieving, or we are harboring unconfessed sin, or we haven't hid enough of the Word in our hearts. We're thwarting God's purpose for ourselves as his children, foolishly settling for second best when we could have so much more. Popular among some fundamentalist media personalities, this version of Christian success is often sold by those who combine their faith with a political conservatism.

We should be aware, however, that this approach to success isn't limited to its extreme form. Hints of the Gospel of Prosperity can be seen in the common assumptions of many in Christian circles.

Many of us wouldn't go so far as the preacher I quoted above, but we do believe God will specially honor the efforts of his people in the workplace. Isn't that why it's confusing when we hear of Christians in business going bankrupt? Especially if they worked hard, were faithful in evangelism, generous to their employees and honest in their dealings?

And what about believers suddenly losing their jobs? Don't the Scriptures promise that God will meet our needs? "My God will meet all your needs according to his glorious riches in Christ Jesus," Paul writes (Phil 4:19). How can this possibly mesh with financial bankruptcy? Don't most of us find ourselves assuming there must be something amiss in the lives of these people? Doesn't having needs met imply at least a minimal measure of success?

Last year I spoke to a small group in Colorado for whom

some of these questions were very real indeed. Made up of couples between thirty and fifty years of age, many of them had experienced a sudden loss of income within the last twelve months. Some had been laid-off from positions they'd previously thought God had blessed them with. Others had watched once thriving small businesses go belly up. They told me how not so long ago they'd praised God for these jobs which most had assumed would provide for their families right into retirement. They realized the economy of the entire state had been hit hard with the collapse of the oil industry, but that failed to satisfy. Sure, their basic needs were met, since their fellow believers had rallied around them—nobody in the group was malnourished. Still, they wondered, where was God in all of this? Why hadn't he provided work when they had spent months scouring the job market? Why hadn't he answered their prayers? Were they being punished?

Success and the God of the Poor

The Gospel of Simple Living, on the other hand, appears to slide to the other end of the spectrum. This message is also buttressed with biblical texts, but of a different flavor.

> Looking at his disciples, [Jesus] said: "*Blessed are you who are poor*, for yours is the kingdom of God." (Lk 6:20, emphasis mine)

> In fact, *everyone* who wants to live a godly life in Christ Jesus *will be persecuted*. (2 Tim 3:12, emphasis mine)

> *Sell your possessions and give to the poor*. Provide purses for yourselves that will not wear out, a *treasure in heaven* that will not be exhausted, where no thief comes near and no moth destroys. For where your treasure is, there your heart will be also. (Lk 12:33-34, emphasis mine)

These Scriptures, it's claimed, are obvious to all who take the Bible seriously and who refuse to fall into the fundamentalist trap of selective interpretation. God is the God of the poor. If Christians really submit to Christ's lordship, hard times are sure to result, since the ways of God are so different from the standards of the world. Our Lord was poor and his disciples are called to follow his example. How can we possibly indulge in the good things of life when we live in a world that is full of suffering and starvation? If we are wealthy, it means we are not sharing equitably the earth's dwindling resources. Being part of Western culture means being part of an economic system that exploits and oppresses the poor.

As one spokesman for the Gospel of Simple Living puts it, "The Third World is poor *because* we are rich." This strikes a chord from childhood. "Remember the starving in India," my folks would always say as they told me to finish my dinner. God's success for us is in the pursuit of social justice. This depth of soul releases a person from the cares of this life and yields a freedom that is unknown in the rat race of the marketplace. To miss this truth is to have a lack of compassion, and our Western affluence is a mark of our guilt. Popular among some Christian intellectuals, this second version of Christian success is often pronounced by those who define their synthesis of faith and political liberalism as prophetic.

This version of success also shows up in subtler forms. Most of us are not as extreme as the speaker I quoted above, but we do tend to feel guilty when we see pictures of starving children. Or we joke that something "is so much fun it must be sinful." And don't we get a bit nervous when everything seems to be going too smoothly?

A friend of mine, who just finished university, wrote recently to tell me about the job he would start at the end of the summer. "I should not enjoy my calling as much as I do," he wrote. Somehow it wouldn't seem godly to have a job that was a delight. We often speak of finding God's will in negative terms. Whatever his will is, we probably won't like it.

One woman who was serving with a mission organization in Europe claims this is all really very simple. People are perishing in this fallen world, and nothing else matters. Comfort can wait for heaven. "I can tell instantly when I'm starting to fall into sin," she said. "When I start to rearrange the cardboard boxes and trunks in our tent I know I have to beware. I'm starting to get concerned about worldly matters."

And after all, don't the Scriptures claim that hardship is the Christian's lot? "For it has been granted to you on behalf of Christ not only to believe on him, but also to suffer for him," Paul wrote (Phil 1:29). How can this possibly mesh with financial security? Don't we assume there must be something amiss when we meet Christians who are wealthy? And isn't it unsettling when weeks go by without major difficulty for us, while Christians in the Third World starve, suffer and die?

Success by Default
The Gospel of Prosperity and the Gospel of Simple Living are so popular among Christians that they tend to dominate any discussion on success. Their message is spread in magazines, seminars and journals. Not surprisingly, the Simple Livers and the Prosperitans aren't very impressed with each other. Sometimes they're not even convinced they hold Christianity in common.

These two versions of Christian success compete for our attention and can seem to make life more complicated than it already is. We can feel pulled in opposite directions, even if we aren't really convinced we should follow either one.

Several years ago my wife and I decided we would like to purchase a piece of sculpture. It was made by a Christian friend and seemed to express something of the beauty and wonder of the joy of being alive in the world God had made. We wanted to buy it, but the decision raised important issues since commissioning a bronze sculpture is an expensive proposition. Could we justify such a purchase in a hungry world? Does agreeing with Simple Livers in a *concern* for the poor rule out the possibility of owning such a piece of art? On the other hand, does not the artist have the right to make a living with his work? Would exhibiting this art in our living room make Prosperitans assume we were one of them? We could imagine the Christians from both sides arguing about what we should decide to do. And they would probably come to opposite conclusions. And both would claim to have the Word of God on *their* side.

My intention here has not been to exhaustively outline and analyze these competing versions. That would require a book in itself. Rather, my goal has been to try to capture something of the mindset I believe these two approaches have spawned in the minds of many believers. Torn between two poles, they feel assaulted from both sides, but aided by neither.

Though the Prosperity and Simple Living Gospels tend to receive the most press, many don't accept either option. In fact, they are mirror images of each other, and I'm convinced they're both erroneous.[1] Both of these theories tend to treat the measures of success—their presence or their absence—as measures of people and their spirituality. Judgments of faithfulness are made by focusing on conformity to or against material and cultural norms. Certainly both of these theories contain elements of truth, but there is clearly something missing. Although believers may be quite sure they disagree with these two versions, they're often less sure of what to replace them with. And if they don't develop a vigorous biblical perspective—and most don't—they end up with Success by Default.

Success by Default is the third Christian version of success. There are some things we can be sure about, it is claimed. We should be upright, hard working and spiritual—there really can't be much debate about that. Then, apparently, whatever follows will be fine, since it will be God's blessing. Surely that's success enough.

That sounds fine when discussed at weekend retreats, but this version of success has its problems. It's so ambiguous that it turns out to be of little practical help. How are we to recognize this blessing-as-success when it arrives? How are we to apply this to what we face in the workplace? And when does "hard working" begin to mean "joining the rat race"?

Second, Success by Default is not really an alternative, but merely a rejection of the other two more radical versions of Christian success. Is this the most we can come up with for something as important as success? Obedience for Christians involves action, holy action, not simply reaction.

Finally, Success by Default is insufficient because it doesn't provide a clear vision of success to pursue. Thus it isn't vigorous enough to guard us from simply absorbing the views around us. Such an approach is unbecoming to the disciple. Obedience doesn't consist of following the crowd, even when the crowd quotes Scripture.

Success and Faithfulness

The definition of success that we adopt is an important part of our world view. It's part of our understanding of life, of worldliness and of true spirituality. And it will be judged when we stand before our Creator. It would be wise to be sure our perspectives on success and failure are in line with the mind and heart of our Lord.

The Gospel of Prosperity, the Gospel of Simple Living and Success by Default are inadequate solutions for Christians. We aren't given a simplistic formula in the Scriptures to plug in their place. The Bible's concept of success is far richer than that.

"Be faithful," the Lord Christ commands, "even to the point of death" (Rev 2:10). We can think Christianly about success and failure by wrestling with what it means to be faithful to our Master. On this side of heaven we'll never manage this with perfection, but we aren't left in the dark to grope aimlessly. The Scriptures give us clear principles from which we can hammer out the specifics of faithfulness in a fallen world. For Christians the issue of success and failure is inextricably tied up in what it means to be faithful to our Lord and Savior, Jesus Christ.

Thinking and acting Christianly about success and faithfulness takes on added significance in a culture that has elevated success to the status of the divine. Our society's idea of success is attractive and seductive, and we'd better understand it if we're to live faithfully in our generation. It's to this cultural understanding of success that we turn in the next chapter.

Questions for Individuals and Groups

1. In order to allow the proponents of the Gospel of Prosperity and the Gospel of Simple Living to speak for themselves, track down articles explaining their perspectives. Go through them carefully. Where do you agree? disagree? Why?

2. Try to define your understanding of success in one sentence. What

does it imply concerning what is most significant or meaningful to you?

3. What are the implications of your view of success for your personal life? your family life? your professional life? your church life? your retirement years?

4. To what extent have your perspectives on success and failure been a version of Success by Default?

5. What influences tended to form your opinions on the topic?

6. What areas of your life or thinking would become clearer if you had a concise biblical definition of success and failure?

7. How have these three versions of success tended to influence approaches to evangelism and missions?

Where are the strengths and weaknesses in each case?

8. How is it that different Christians (such as Simple Livers and Prosperitans) can arrive at such different interpretations of Scripture?

What does this fact imply about our approach to Bible study?

Excellence is thought to be a matter of skill, ability, knowledge or effort. In fact, it is not. Excellence in all cases is a matter of being excellent. When you take an honest, uncomplicated look at those you know who possess the qualities of excellence, creativity, competence and achievement, clearly they are simply being excellent, being creative, being competent, being able. It's really as simple as that.
Werner Erhard

O happiness! Our being's end and aim!
Good, pleasure, ease, content! Whate'er thy name:
That something still which prompts the eternal sigh,
For which we bear to live, or dare to die.
Alexander Pope

In the affluent society no useful distinction can be made between luxuries and necessaries.
John K. Galbraith

CHAPTER 3

THE WORLD'S MEASURE OF SUCCESS

It's not difficult to identify our culture's definition of success. Even if we've never seen it written out, we've probably watched people live it, if only in films or books.[1]

Consider the story of Susan Wolfson.[2] Ten years ago, after finishing an undergraduate degree in history, Susan moved to New York City. She was determined to "make it." After two years of odd jobs, things began to happen. She became production assistant for *Family Circle* magazine, and then a year later she married a journalist. Their combined incomes allowed them a comfortable standard of living. Susan found she was now content at home, but she wasn't satisfied with her career. She wanted more out of her work: "I was looking for something to sink my teeth into . . . I wanted to pick a ladder and move on it."[3]

Later that year she moved to Rowland's, a public relations firm, and her salary doubled. "It was fast," she recalls. "Women were running everywhere. They talked faster. They moved faster."[4] As an executive, new clothes and manicures became a necessity. She was "making an investment in an image," she said.[5]

Rowland's gave her several big accounts to manage—first *Esquire,* and later, *Cosmopolitan.* Increasingly, Susan's life was consumed by her work. "I picked up the signals. . . . If you had a peaceful day, you were a loser. . . . I was working 24 hours. . . . I took it with me wherever I went."[6]

Susan received a large salary increase, but then *Cosmopolitan* suddenly withdrew its account. That didn't bode well for the future, and did nothing to lessen the pressure that was already part of her daily routine. Rowland's, however, assigned Susan to another big client. Then she broke her ankle, but couldn't take time off—there was too much to be done. Rowland's gave her a large bonus—and yet another big account to manage.

Susan loved her work and relished the challenge of it all. Still, there was a cost. It was a relief when friends broke appointments and when her husband worked late. Christmas was swallowed in a swirl of busyness. A special weekend away with her husband had to be canceled. She spent the three days on the phone working on a special public relations project for one of her clients. Adding injury to insult, the event was a disaster.

The next year Susan was promoted yet again, and with the promotion came increased demands. Her birthday found her arriving late to a dinner date with her husband. Then Rowland's added yet another big account for Susan to cover. She tried to turn down the extra work, but the corporate decision had been made. It was a vicious cycle: the better she did, the more she was given to do. So, ordering a new executive calendar planning system, Susan plunged ahead. Come what may, she couldn't allow herself to fail.

Insomnia became a problem, and unwinding seemed impossible. Her mind never left the office. She was given another five-thousand-dollar increase, but that did little to relieve the stress that was her constant companion.

On the shuttle back to New York, Susan assessed her life. She was a successful public relations agent married to a successful newspaperman. Their joint successes enabled them to live in a certain style. Susan traveled with Hartmann luggage. At Charivari, salesgirls knew her by name. During the week, she ate at places like the Quilted Giraffe and Le Zinc. Every five weeks, she had another $70 hairstyle from Charles Fremolaro. She now had four Hermes scarves. Fresh flowers filled her home. Lejaby and Fernando Sanchez were the names on her lingerie. There was a VCR in her den. A bundle of credit cards fit smartly into a Louis Vuitton case. Her body was toned by Nautilus. On average, her monthly American Express bill ran to $1,500. And, recently, she had been pricing a Rolex watch, a Barry Kieselstein-Cord belt, and a country house.

"I couldn't believe how sucked in I was," she recalls. "I felt I'd blinked and it had happened."

While she worked very hard for all the things she wanted, she remained unsatisfied with her life. She remembers telling herself that no matter how much harder she worked or how much higher she climbed, she would never get any closer to having what she needed.

"I wasn't the kind of friend I wanted to be, I wasn't the kind of wife I wanted to be, I was consumed," she recalls. "I started realizing that Having It All was like a dog chasing his tail. I ended up having very little.'"[7]

Knowing that Rowland's was considering making her a vice-president, Susan decided to quit. She knew the promotion signalled success, but she decided it wasn't worth it.

Although Susan Wolfson's experience is more extreme than what most of us have gone through, we can learn from her story. It illustrates two points which are important for the task of thinking Christianly about success. First, Susan's story nicely captures how the Western world usually defines success. Second, it reminds us that Success is a very demanding, even deadly, master. Let's look more closely at both of these points.

What is our world's definition of success? What is it that so many are striving for? To give an answer to this question is not to suggest that there aren't variations to be found. Society is too pluralistic for that. Different ethnic, religious and familial backgrounds make a profound difference in how people come to define what is significant to them.[8]

Nevertheless, most people I've asked seem to have little trouble identifying the predominant version in society: *Success means attaining some measure of money, fame, power and self-fulfillment— and then looking the part.*[9] Let's look at each one of these "five horsemen of success," which embody our aspirations and are driven by our society's commercialism.

Success: Money

The measure of success that probably comes most quickly to mind is money or wealth. Don't we expect an ever-growing standard of living? Workers denied a rise usually complain about unfair employers rather than assess their value or productivity as employees. An increasing standard of living is so taken for granted that most see it as a right.

When it comes to income, we simply could use more. Have you noticed how expenditures seem to expand, taking up all the available money? There's always something to buy. Besides, spending money can be cathartic. For me, browsing in a good bookshop always seems to help when I'm depressed. Recently some friends gave me a seventy-five-dollar book token. I may not be depressed for months.

Advertising and the media confirm the message: successful people have money and things—and in abundance. It feels beggarly to always have to worry about a budget. With success comes the delicious freedom to purchase.

One advertisement sells houses with the slogan: "You've made your success—now live it!" Some products are promoted as the best precisely because they're the most expensive. There's even a chewing gum marketed "for the very rich." An airline ticket agent recently noticed the fountain pen I carry. He seemed a little embarrassed with his Bic. "A touch of class," he commented.

Centering life around money and things makes some sense in an age like ours. When Carl Sagan says "the Cosmos is all that is or ever was or ever will be," he's expressing the belief that reality is limited to the material.[10] Within the narrow confines of this naturalistic world view, the only possible reference point for meaning is material. To embrace materialism, then, follows quite easily. Money is transformed into Mammon and the idolatrous quest begins. Meaning is reduced to affluence, "an overwhelming and ever-increasing prosperity—a life made up of things, things, and more things—a success judged by an ever-higher level of material abundance."[11]

Success: Fame

If a measure of wealth is the first part of the definition of success, fame is a close second. Being on top means there's at least a few peons down below looking up wistfully. There's something exhilarating about being the best.

Recognition, fame, popularity, being known—these are all part of our culture's idea of success. "Success in our society," Christopher Lasch says, "has to be ratified by publicity."[12] Isn't that why magazines run features on people who reach the top? A measure of fame says we've succeeded in "making it."

Of course, some of us assume we're unlike the masses—*we're* not enamored with fame. I used to think I'd treat a famous person just like I'd treat anyone else. After all, being a Christian means every person is equal before God. Of course, at the time I didn't know anyone even remotely famous. Then I had a chance to study at L'Abri Fellowship. Its founder, Francis Schaeffer, was well known by that time. But, I reminded myself, I'm an adult. I'm self-confident. I meet strangers easily. I was sure *I* would not act like some pitiful groupie.

It didn't help that I was engrossed in washing dishes when Dr. Schaeffer suddenly showed up in the kitchen. A nearby L'Abri worker introduced us. It was embarrassing: my mind went blank. I couldn't think of anything to say. I think I told him I was pleased to be there (twice), mentioned my name (twice—after the worker had already mentioned it), and started to mumble something about one of his books (but couldn't remember the title) until my voice just drifted off. Dr. Schaeffer, a very gracious man, made me welcome and then moved on to talk with someone else. The L'Abri worker told me later he had assured Dr. Schaeffer that I was capable, at least on certain days, of speaking in complete sentences.

The fact is, fame captivates us, and along with wealth, it's an integral part of today's version of success.

Success: Power

Power or authority is the third aspect of our culture's definition of success. Sometimes these perks come packaged together. Imagine: a promotion with a healthy rise, increased authority and a bigger office with your name engraved on a bronze plaque on the door. If that isn't success in today's world, what is?

Part of my work involves speaking at weekend conferences. Have you noticed how The Speaker has authority simply by being the speaker? Christians actually treat The Speaker differently from everyone else. The Speaker can ask to have the chairs rearranged (by others), and is seldom signed up to do kitchen duty. And then, regardless of your topic or area of expertise, a few will seek your opinion on everything from nuclear weapons to child rearing. Suddenly, by being The Speaker, I have authority to address all topics. The fact that truth, not opinion, should be the Christian's concern is apparently forgotten.

Still, it makes me feel good when they ask. It's a form of power that is intoxicating to me. I have felt the seduction of the quest for authority and power as a measure of success.

Success: Self-fulfillment

Besides wealth, fame and power, self-fulfillment is also prominent in the Western idea of success. This emphasis is actually relatively new. Only a generation or two back, people didn't list self-fulfillment as part of their vision of success. The change this represents is great enough that social scientists refer to it as "the leading edge of a genuine cultural revolution."[13]

What's happened is that a shift has occurred in what is known as the "giving/getting compact." These are "the unwritten rules governing what we give in marriage, work, community and sacrifice for others, and what we expect in return."[14] In other words, what we demand from life has changed from previous generations. And that has altered our view of success.

This came home to me several years ago during a visit to my grandfather. Now in his eighties, Grandfather Haack still holds the old notion of the giving/getting compact. It could be summarized something like this:

> I give hard work, loyalty and steadfastness. I swallow my frustrations and suppress my impulse to do what I would enjoy, and do what is expected of me instead. I do not put myself first; I put the needs of others ahead of my own. I give a lot, but what I get in return is worth it. I receive an ever-growing standard of living, and a family life with a devoted spouse and decent kids. Our children will take care of us in our old age if we really need it, which thank goodness we will not. I have a nice home, a good job, the respect of my friends and neighbors; a sense of accomplishment at having made something of my life. Last but not least, as an American I am proud to be a citizen of the finest country in the world.[15]

If that sounds foreign it's because of the transformation our expectations about life have undergone. The conviction has grown that this old compact sacrificed too much, and received too little in return. Such self-denial is no longer seen as worthwhile, or necessary.

So the compact has been altered: self-fulfillment was added. As social scientist Daniel Yankelovich puts it:

> On traditional demands for material well-being seekers of

self-fulfillment now impose new demands for intangibles—creativity, leisure, autonomy, pleasure, participation, community, adventure, vitality, stimulation, tender loving care. To the efficiency of technological society they wish to add joy of living. They seek to satisfy both the body *and* the spirit. . . .[16]

For some, self-fulfillment has become more important than wealth, power or fame. Some executives have resigned their positions—as Susan Wolfson did—moved to the country and found less stressful, but more satisfying work.

Don't most of us want a job that is both satisfying and that provides a sufficient income? Don't we cherish a position that stimulates us to be creative? Won't we quit our job if another comes along that offers more fulfillment than the one we're in? For most of us, self-fulfillment is part of success.

Success: Appearances

On top of wealth, fame, power and self-fulfillment, success in modern culture means looking successful. It isn't just the acquisition of these status symbols that matters. The appearance of success can be as important as the success itself.[17] It's even possible for failures to become successes by simply looking the part.

Here's an item from a mail-order catalog—the "Power Symbol":

European style yachting bracelet, for the man at the helm. This design is just like the one seen at Milan's most expensive men's jeweler . . . Authentic steel sail cable is bound with lustrous 14K gold, a combination that expresses strength and your appreciation for the finer things of life . . . Wear it on board—or in the boardroom. And see the difference this subtle display of power can make.

All for a cool $299.00.

Books and seminars are available on how to tailor one's physical appearance to achieve "the look of the successful, the celebrated, the select."[18] Dress, posture, office decor, make of car, the restaurants one frequents—all these can broadcast a message of personal success. Sparseness on your desk implies efficiency, but make sure your calendar looks filled—even if you have nothing planned for months.

Interior decorators design offices that will subtly send messages of authority to visitors. One sales training seminar recommends that when at the office of someone you wish to impress, use his phone to make a call. Better yet, have someone call you while you're there. Make it sound important, even if it isn't. Take the call sitting on the edge of his desk, twiddling with his paperweight or pen. Let him watch you make decisions perched up above him, and the momentum of the meeting will shift in your favor.

The issue of appearances doesn't just apply to business executives in smart suits. Faded denim also communicates about one's identity and view of success. Isn't this what we mean when we talk of our lifestyle "making a statement"? How we look matters. And the person who succeeds will not look like a failure.

A measure of wealth, fame, power and self-fulfillment, and the chance to look the part: these compose the predominant definition of success today. Understanding how the world defines success is the first point illustrated by Susan Wolfson's story. If we are to live faithful lives as followers of Jesus Christ, we need to recognize that these are the measures of success and failure adopted by our culture. After all, our faithfulness must be lived out in the midst of it.

Success: An Evaluation

The emphasis on wealth, power, fame, self-fulfillment and appearance are so all-pervasive, it's hard to think what else success might comprise. How should we as Christians evaluate this definition?

It should be obvious that wealth doesn't automatically imply success in the world God has made. Jesus called the rich man who was "not rich toward God" a "fool" (Lk 12:13-21). "Is not life more important than food," Jesus warned, "and the body more important than clothes?" (Mt 6:25).

Fame, too, is hardly a guarantee of success. Christian belief stresses that life is extremely brief (1 Pet 1:24). "The living know that they will die," Ecclesiastes reminds us, ". . . and even the memory of them is forgotten" (9:5). Applause is a wonderful sound, but the ovation of mankind is nothing compared to pleasing God. One is temporal; the other is eternal.

Is being in a place of power a sufficient measure of success? God is on record as laughing at such things (Ps 2:4). Authority over others must be handled with care, the apostle warns, "since you know that he who is both their Master and yours is in heaven, and there is no favoritism with him" (Eph 6:9). Rather than being regarded as a sign of success, the authority that comes our way will be judged by the Master. If we fail at that tribunal, we'll wish we had never had the power in the first place.

It's understandable why creatures made in God's image would desire self-fulfillment. We were created for meaning. As an end in itself, however, the quest for self-fulfillment is an elusive, self-centered pursuit. And what of the warning that we're to "do nothing out of selfish ambition" (Phil 2:3)? Feeling satisfied is hardly the ultimate standard. The rich fool, we are told, was enjoying his "ease" (Lk 12:19).

And lastly, what about the emphasis on the appearance of success? As physical beings, appearances do make a difference in the world God has made. We communicate something of who we are by how we dress. Our office and home say something about how we look at ourselves and life. We are called to image God across all of reality, and that includes an "obedient aesthetic life."[19] Still, faithfulness must mean more than manipulating externals for mere effect. "Man looks at the outward appearance," Scripture tells us, while God "looks at the heart" (1 Sam 16:7).

Malcolm Muggeridge's testimony puts the contemporary view of success within the proper context:

> I may, I suppose, regard myself, or pass for being, a relatively successful man. People occasionally stare at me in the streets—that's fame. I can fairly easily earn enough to qualify for admission to the higher slopes of the Inland Revenue—that's success. Furnished with money and a little fame even the elderly, if they care to, may partake of trendy diversions—that's pleasure. It might happen once in a while that something I said or wrote was sufficiently heeded for me to persuade myself that it represents a serious impact on our time—that's fulfillment. Yet I say to you—and I beg you to believe me—multiply these tiny triumphs by a million, add them all together, and they are nothing—less than nothing, a positive impediment—measured against one draught of that living water Christ offers to the spiritually thirsty, irrespective of who or what they are.[20]

Thinking Christianly about success leads us to conclude that the world's definition is inadequate. Having a measure of wealth, fame, power, self-fulfillment and the appearance of succeeding simply isn't enough. From a Christian perspective, even a total failure can have all these things—even in abundance. That may be noteworthy, but it hardly transforms someone into a success before God.

But success can take on an even more sinister cast than merely being inadequate. The world's success is deeply seductive, and therein lies a great and mortal danger. Offering enchantments we can enjoy no place else, it asks only that we fraternize a little. If we have eyes to see, we'll recognize that its invitation is to frolic in spiritual adultery with a very fickle god. That's the second lesson to be gleaned from Susan Wolfson's story, and the next chapter is devoted to it.

Questions for Individuals and Groups

1. Which of the five measures of success is (are) most attractive to you?

2. What are the dangers in each one?

What practical plans should you make to deal with each weakness?

3. In what ways has the church adopted the culture's approach to success? What are Christian versions of success-as-money? Success-as-fame? Success-as-power? Success-as-self-fulfillment? Success-as-appearance?

4. What strategies (physical or spiritual) can we develop to train our children to look beyond the culture's definition of success and failure?

5. Read Walker Percy's excellent novel, *The Second Coming* (Granada, 1985). How does the author use success and failure as a theme? How does he question the prevalent cultural notions? What does he suggest in their place? Is this a sufficient alternative?

6. Collect and examine magazine (or TV) ads for various products. What do they suggest or reinforce concerning notions of success and failure?

7. Are there positive ways in which God could use each of the five measures of success in a Christian's life?

How can you justify your ideas here biblically?

8. Is there evidence that our society recognizes the inherent weaknesses in its definition of success? Explain.

How might Christians be able to use this to bring healing and good news into lives?

Looks aren't everything.
Luxury's not everything.
Money's not everything.
Health is not everything.
Success is not everything.
Happiness is not everything.
Even everything is not everything.
There's more to life than everything.
Steve Turner

The moral flabbiness born of the bitch-goddess SUCCESS.
That—with the squalid cash interpretation put on the
word success—is our national disease.
William James

Prosperity doth bewitch men, seeming clear;
But seas do laugh, show white, when rocks are near.
John Webster

CHAPTER 4

WHERE SUCCESS AND IDOLATRY MEET

*F*or all its appeal, success can be a demanding, even a deadly master. There's a fine line between being on a successful career track and being caught up in a rat race that's out of control. This is the second point illustrated by Susan Wolfson's story from the last chapter.

For many, the pursuit of the world's standards of success has become identical to finding meaning in life. That shouldn't really surprise us. What else do people have to live for? For decades professors and the media have championed the secular myth, proclaiming the here and now is all there is. "You were born without purpose," Swedish film director Ingmar Bergman writes, "you live with meaning, living is its own meaning. When you die, you are extinguished. From being you will be transformed to non-being."[1] If you believe that, there's no reason why you shouldn't lose yourself in a life dedicated to art or the theater, or why you shouldn't take up the challenge of conquering the business world by getting to the top. Giving yourself to success at any cost can be an exhilarating challenge. If you only go around once, can you think of any reason why you shouldn't grab for all the gusto?

The tragedy, of course, is that this is the path of death. Life can only be meaningful if lived in reference to the God of life. If we do not bow before him, we have bowed before another, false god. To understand the dynamics of success as a life-encompassing quest, we must learn to think in terms of idolatry. Success can be made a god.

Though the Scriptures have a great deal to say about idolatry, most Christians understand it poorly. That's why we find the accounts of false worship in Scripture difficult to comprehend. Were the Israelites so primitive as to think a metal calf rescued them from slavery in Egypt (Ex 32)? Were the Old Testament worshipers of idols so ignorant they believed a statue could hear their prayers (1 Kings 18; Dan 3)?

But idolatry has nothing to do with being primitive or modern, and a high IQ is no guarantee we'll worship the true and living God. To turn *from* God is the nature of sin. But we always turn *toward* something as we turn away from God (Rom 1:18-25). To discover what we have turned to is to identify our idol.

We all order our lives—our choices, priorities and values—around something. If our lives are not centered in God and his truth, then they will be centered in something else. This "something else" is the false god we worship. Thus, "idolatry in its larger meaning is properly understood as any substitution of what is created for the creator."[2]

How can we tell if we're being tempted by idolatry? By taking seriously the command not to covet. Covetousness is a form of idolatry (Col 3:5). An idol is any object of ardent devotion, anything that has been made the center of our heart's desire. "If only I had education or money or looks or success—then I'd be happy, fulfilled, complete." This is the language of idolatry, the language of covetousness. Instead of trusting in God who is the only source of good, our trust has been placed in the created thing from which the desired good can never come.

An idol becomes to some extent the norm and inspiration for life, the reference point for happiness, significance or meaning. Rather than submitting to God, the person submits to the values and priorities that emanate from the object that's been transformed into an image of devotion.

Idolatry must not be understood primarily in terms of cultic rituals, such as bowing before an icon. Many modern idols aren't clothed in religious dress. The fact that one idolatry involves religious ritual (Baal) and another doesn't (Success) is really secondary. In each case, something has usurped the place of God. If they were convinced it would multiply their effectiveness, the followers of Success-as-god would probably be happy to engage in some sort of ritual. The reason they do not is that today many people see science, not religion, as the best tool for making it in life.

The Attractiveness of False Gods
Since Paul identified covetousness as idolatry, we should be alert to the danger of this sin. False gods are profoundly seductive in a fallen world. The idols of each age may be unique to that period, but all false gods are attractive in three important ways.

Idolatry is attractive, first, because people want to be like everyone else around them. Even nonconformists are usually conforming to some group. We have a desire to be accepted and appreciated. Nobody likes being different all the time. Isn't it true at work, for example? Don't we want our supervisors and colleagues to think well of the job we do—and of us?

The problem arises when we are increasingly tempted to order our lives around the same values and things (idols) as those whom we want to impress. It's a short step from desiring acceptance to sharing their perspectives, priorities and affections. After all, we have to work with them thirty-five or more hours a week. We can hardly hope to be promoted if we don't "fit in." Before we realize it, this process can become the subtle first step to idolatry.

Idolatry is seductive, secondly, because it is easier to trust something physical than it is to trust God. It's easy to talk about faith in God, but when our backs are against the wall, it can be hard to practice. *Things* are easier to focus on. The Canaanites worshiped a physical object in their temple. The Israelites had to take God's word for it that he was there behind the veil.

When Samuel grew old, he appointed his sons to succeed him as judges of Israel. But they were dishonest and untrustworthy, so the people began to ask Samuel for a king. "This displeased Samuel; so he prayed to the LORD. And the LORD told him: 'Listen to . . . the people; . . . it is not you they have rejected, but they have rejected me as their king' " (1 Sam 8:6-7). Because of their desire for a physical king (to "be like all the other nations," v. 20), the Israelites forfeited the protection and privileges offered by the true King.

The tangible or physical can seem more solid, somehow more trustworthy. We see this with our income. "Trusting God for our finances" sounds wonderful, but a signed contract with a hefty rise from a large corporation can feel far more secure. "Believing he will provide" is a good topic for a weekend retreat, but a healthy pension plan and life assurance make the future seem less scary. It's not that we don't wish to walk by faith. It's that the tangible appears more real, more dependable, easier to trust. This struggle can be the opening wedge to idolatry.

Third, idolatry is attractive because at times idols seem to produce. Do we think the ancient pagans never gave testimonies? Modern Philistines do. The marketplace is glutted with voices proclaiming that the all-consuming pursuit of success can yield substantial rewards. Success may be a false god, but it certainly isn't a powerless one.

Just look at what can be yours: clothes, cars, money, sex—the list is almost endless. This is what Success promises. Doesn't it seem that the ones who sell their souls to the company reap much in a fun lifestyle? Don't we find that at all attractive—even a little?

Success as Lord

Once we understand the nature of idolatry, it's easy to see how Success can be made a god. The process is deceptively simple. And it is seductively attractive. Wealth, fame, power or self-fulfillment take the place of God. And covetousness puts them there. Success is not only offered to us, it is said to be good.

Scripture says we become like the object of our adoration.[3] Worship an idol, and this false reference point will begin to define our values and choices. When Success is made a god, its followers begin to judge life, people and events according to its demands and perspectives. We may dislike someone or refuse friendship with them because they are not successful. We may even mistreat our family if our success requires it.

Or consider power: as Lord Acton pointed out, "power tends to corrupt, and absolute power corrupts absolutely." Too often in this fallen world "power holders start to exploit those they control; they become puffed up with their own importance; their moral values become self-serving."[4] Just as the morality in the myths surrounding Baal influenced the life and choices of his devotees, so the modern god Success transforms its follower's ethics.

John was one of the leaders of the Christian fellowship group in medical school. An active believer, he was also deeply committed to excellence in his profession. But after graduation John's priorities slowly began to change. Increasingly he poured himself into his work to the exclusion of everything else. Other priorities and concerns, he would always say, "will be handled later, as soon as I'm respected in my field." Respect came, along with wealth and the authority which normally is given to physicians, but somehow it was never enough.

I don't know John's heart, but I do know something of the agony his wife Judy has gone through. Increasingly John has exhibited the values, priorities and choices of a person whose heart is more attuned to Success than to Christ. In fact, John does not even claim to be a Christian anymore. Bring up any topic except his career or belongings, and he will change the subject. Only the Lord can say whether John has turned from God to Success, but the characteristic marks of idolatry are there.

Secret Infiltration

Idols like Success are dangerous because they mask their true nature, slipping in quietly like spies secretly infiltrating behind enemy lines. Believers can be overwhelmed because the false god does not arrive with trumpets and fanfare—if it did, we would spot it in a moment. They seduce us because they creep in silently, never seeming to be as foreign or as evil as they truly are.

This quiet infiltration sometimes occurs as a distortion of true religion. Remember how Moses constructed a serpent of bronze at God's command when the camp was overrun by snakes as a judgment of God (Num 21)? Those who looked at the bronze snake were healed of any bites they received from the invading snakes. Eight centuries later King Hezekiah had to destroy the metal object because the people were burning incense to it (2 Kings 18:4).

This could have come about as a slow process involving a series of small, seemingly innocuous choices. Perhaps they kept the snake initially as a reminder of God's holiness and judgment. Incense could have been added later as a teaching aid, to make each visit more memorable. Before long people began to feel it was more meaningful, more spiritual somehow, to pray before the snake than at home. And so it went, until the bronze serpent became Nehushtan, an idol a righteous king had to destroy for the glory of God.

My friend John from medical school did not get where he is today by suddenly leaping up and embracing paganism. One of the things the medical school fellowship had discussed was the need for Christians to fulfill their callings to God's glory. Shoddy workmanship and sloppy standards would not do. Could it be that, like the Israelites and the bronze snake, John began with good plans, but then slowly moved off track? Could he have mistaken the adoration of Success for the pursuit of Christian excellence?

The fact that we live in a culture so enthralled with Success should make us cautious. Surrounded by idols, we can begin to think of them as natural—and even a little appealing. Is it surprising that in a secularized culture Success is so tempting? It promises a great deal. All one has to give is worship. "Make me the center of your heart's desire," Success murmurs, "and I'll throw open the windows of my heaven and pour out so much blessing that you'll not have room to spare."

Rubbish-Dump Quiet Times and Other Strategies for Dethroning the Idol of Success

What is the Christian response to the dynamic which animates the pursuit of Success-as-god? Modern society has elevated this pursuit to divine heights. Transformed by idolatry, people have begun worshiping Success-as-god. What does it mean to act Christianly when we are surrounded by idols? I would suggest four responses.

First, we need to clearly understand the nature and meaning of idolatry. This will occur only if our thinking is informed by a serious study of Scripture. As the first two commandments suggest, we will need both to know God deeply, and to identify and flee false gods.

It's important that we develop skill in recognizing the idols around us. We must understand the cultural dynamics of success to be able to discern right and wrong. We can be like the men of Issachar "who understood the times and knew what Israel should do" (1 Chron 12:32). The forms of worldliness that are most dangerous are not those which are obvious. Most dangerous are the subtle ideas that slip in without notice. Many who would be appalled at adultery or gambling, for example, are unfortunately captive to the mindset of the world concerning success and failure.[5] But we must learn to keep ourselves from the modern idol of Success (1 Jn 5:21).

Second, as the Spirit convicts us, we must identify those pressure points at which we are tempted. That will not make our struggles disappear, but it is wise to be aware of our weaknesses. And, where necessary, we must confess our sin and repent of our covetousness.

It is good to remember that our Master understands the struggle. The Lord Jesus is no stranger to the temptations of recognition (Mt 4:1-3), power and fame (vv. 5-6), and riches and authority (vv. 8-9). Our temptation will never catch him off guard. Never will our sin elicit a gasp of surprise from our High Priest, though it might call forth his discipline.

I think all Christians should regularly visit the city rubbish dump. Have a quiet time there. Spend some time in the Scriptures and in prayer, preferably with your car window open. As you do so, remind yourself of what is around you. In huge rotting piles is the accumulated stuff which some have lived for, and perhaps even died for. By God's grace may we be saved from ash-heap lives.[6]

Third, we must be concerned for the havoc that is being wreaked in so many lives by the pursuit of Success. Seldom has an idol extracted so great a price and given so little in return. In opposition to this bondage, the story of the Scriptures is indeed good news.

Human beings were made to be in relationship with God. When the center of life is shifted to something smaller and meaner, the outcome will be poor. Cultural success—growing prosperity, fame, power and self-fulfillment—does not bring *shalom;* it does not bring peace. To make these things the measure of life is to build upon sand. When *U.S. News and World*

Report ran a cover story on the topic of success, they included a warning: "This latest love affair with success—when pursued with single-minded purpose—could exact a big toll in the form of sickness, career problems, neglected children and broken families."[7]

The call to offer the gospel to those who have elevated Success to god-status is a great challenge. We must "speak the uncompromising word of truth in love to a sector [of Western society] who glory in what the Scriptures call shame."[8]

Last, we must develop a biblical alternative to our culture's understanding of success. Faithfulness before God means a living exhibition of life lived under Christ's lordship. Accomplishing this by God's grace will be a bracing affair. "Show that to the heathen," Dorothy Sayers wrote, "and they may not believe it; but at least they may realize that here is something that a man might be glad to believe."[9]

We must live faithfully under Christ's lordship because his glory is at stake. We need to recover a holy jealousy for the true God. Are we unmoved when tin gods like Success claim an allegiance that is due only to the Creator? It's right to be angry that such impostors leave in their wake the debris of broken lives and cultures. Whether we destroy the false altars quietly as Gideon did (Judg 6:27) or openly as Elijah did (1 Kings 18:16-40) is not important. What is vital is that for the glory of our God they be pulled down.

Herbert Schlossberg correctly summed up the challenge before us in this way:

> One reason Chesterton's writings have been so challenging and hopeful to three generations of Christians is that he captured better than most the quality of adventure in Christian life. That is a quality of which we shall have more than

enough if we are willing to accomplish the task that lies before us. For even the good kings of ancient Judah, who expelled the worship of the Baals from the temple, left the Asherim and their devotees undisturbed on the hills. So rooted in communal life had these deities become, that it was unthinkable to be rid of them. In the late twentieth century the West is similarly plagued with major and minor idols, some of them all but invisible. It is hard to imagine a more important or satisfying role than to embark on the spiritual, intellectual, and political adventure of working toward stripping them, root and branch, from the land.[10]

Our society's definition of success is insufficient at best, blasphemous at worst. The inadequacy of Western cultural success is made even clearer when we examine the lives of those who are on record as having pleased God. Not surprisingly, God's assessment does not always resonate with modern conclusions. And it is to that subject that we turn in the next chapter.

Questions for Individuals or Groups

1. What do Genesis 1:27, Psalm 115:2-8 and 2 Corinthians 3:12-18 indicate about the relationship between people and the object of their worship?
   Why do people tend to become like what they worship?

2. How do those who pursue money, power, fame, self-fulfillment and appearance become like the object of their pursuit?

3. What do we find particularly attractive about success?
   How can we be sure that hasn't started to become covetousness?

4. Study the stories of Gideon and Elijah in Judges 6 and 1 Kings 18. What can we learn from their example of defeating false gods?

5. In what ways might Christians be involved in toppling Success-as-god?

6. What will be required of us if we're to do this with integrity?
   What costs might be involved?

7. How would you explain the Christian perspective of success as idolatry to a thinking non-Christian?
   Could it be done in a way that they could understand? Why or why not?

8. Draw together materials from the media or the non-Christian press which point out dangers in the all-encompassing pursuit of success. To what extent do these echo the Christian's concerns? To what extent do they differ?

Countless acts by millions of self-centered,
instead of God-centered, individuals may reasonably be
thought to be destroying the world.
G. K. Chesterton

Prosperity is the blessing of the Old Testament,
adversity is the blessing of the New.
Francis Bacon

There is a legitimate and God-inspired sense of pride
in self-worth. But what we see in magazines, like the one
named *Self,* is something else: it is either rebellion declaring
itself, or despair whistling in the dark.
Richard Lovelace

CHAPTER 5

CASE STUDIES IN THE FAILURE OF SUCCESS

*E*lisabeth Elliot had every reason to wonder about the success of her life as a missionary in Ecuador.

Believing they were led by God, Jim and Elisabeth Elliot had gone to South America. In the attempt to evangelize the Auca Indians, Jim and four companions were speared to death on a remote river bank. This loss was only the beginning for Elisabeth Elliot.

Confident the Lord was calling her to do Bible translation work, Elisabeth and her daughter Valery went to live among the Aucas. Within a month her translation helper from the tribe was shot and killed. Undeterred, she forged ahead with learning the language and rendering it in written form. After months of labor, she left her carefully compiled notes with a colleague. Two weeks later they were stolen. No copies existed; the files were never found.[1] She had precious little—except loss—to show for her efforts. Her labor seemed wasted.

How would this rate according to our standards for success? Probably as failure. A bright young couple goes off to the jungle as missionaries. How important could translating the Bible be since the Aucas already had a religion? This intrusion from the outside risked the destruction of the Auca native culture. And in the end, the Elliots' work all came to nothing, and tragedy and disappointment flooded Elisabeth's life. According to our culture's perspective on success, Elisabeth Elliot's story is a lesson in failure. But is this assessment correct?

Success and the God Who Is There
If God exists, talk of success in life is meaningless unless it is related to pleasing him. From this perspective, Elisabeth's story is not a story of failure. She lived before the God who never slumbers nor sleeps. Even as she grieved over her losses she could say with Hezekiah: "Remember, O LORD, how I have walked before you faithfully and with wholehearted devotion and have done what is good in your eyes" (Is 38:3).

This is easier to talk about than to face realistically. Elisabeth first lost her husband, then her translation helper and finally the tangible results of months of hard work. Does her life illustrate a success I'd be content with—especially if achieving it meant I needed to face similar loss repeatedly? Am I willing to live faithfully before God even if it means being dubbed a failure by popular vote?

Her suffering and loss were certainly very real. Still, even in the midst of our ongoing struggle with the results of the Fall, our task as Christians is to please God. Pleasing him—regardless of results or hardship or societal response—must be central to our notion of success. And what pleases God is faithfulness.

The real struggle in life is not between success or failure as they are commonly understood. Rather, what should really grip our minds and hearts and imaginations is the challenge of pleasing God by being faithful across the full scope of our lives.

If God does not exist, then nothing finally matters at all. In our modern age of unbelief, sometimes it has been unbelievers who have seen this most clearly. Ingmar Bergman, the son of a minister, directed a trilogy of films that explore life in a universe without God. With the stark images of cold Scandinavian landscapes for a backdrop, dark scenes spin out a three-fold story of despair.

In *Through a Glass Darkly*, family members hesitantly reach out to each other and wonder if they have achieved love and meaning in their lives. With no assurance that life has purpose, they can't be sure.

In the second film, *Winter Light*, we watch a pastor lose his faith. Slowly, painfully he becomes convinced there is no reason to believe that God exists. The film closes with a haunting image, leaving the viewer with only empty words in the face of death, and no surety in the midst of life. Too weak to face his doubts, the sick and feverish Rev. Eriksson walks to the altar to begin the service of worship in an all-but-empty church. The final words of the soundtrack are the opening lines of the liturgy: "Holy, holy, holy, Lord God Almighty." The eternal hymn of the cherubim becomes a cry of despair.

The final film of the three carries Bergman's message in its title, *The Silence*. If there is no God, silence is all that there is. Silence about meaning, about morality, about success and failure, about life and death.

This bleak picture is the true backdrop for any discussion about purpose and meaning in life. If there is no God, then wrangling over success and failure is nothing more than a joke. But if God exists, then our questions about success and failure are inextricably linked with what it means to live as though God is there. How do we live faithfully before him? Ultimately, nothing else matters.

Thankfully, the universe is not coldly silent, and mankind, though fallen, is not stillborn. God exists and has spoken. Having been given his Word, we have a standard by which to live. In the Bible we find stories of some who pleased God and stories of some who didn't. Such character studies won't yield all we need to know concerning faithfulness or success and failure. They will, however, bring some of the key principles into sharper relief. We'll look at three: Jeremiah, a list of heroes in Hebrews 11 and Solomon.

In each case, we'll want to consider the following questions as we proceed:

1. What was it in this individual's life that caused him to be pleasing—or displeasing—to God?

2. What relationship did pleasing (or displeasing) God have to wealth, fame, power, self-fulfillment and appearance?

3. Would this individual be considered a success or failure today? Why? Does it matter?

4. What does it mean to please God? How can we live faithfully today? Are we willing to?

Jeremiah: Sinking in the Mire

The sixth century B.C. saw an extraordinary group of thinkers at work: Lao-tse and Confucius in China, Gautama Buddha in India, Thales and Pythagoras in Ionia, and Zoroaster in Persia.[2] It was an age of great ideas and religious activity. It was in this period that God raised up a thinker and prophet in Israel. Jeremiah brought God's word to God's people, and lived to see the fading days of a great and noble culture.

We're introduced to Jeremiah as he receives a call from God. Though he already has a career set out before him, Jeremiah is interrupted in his plans. The young priest from Judah is to be "a prophet to the nations" (Jer 1:5). Jeremiah isn't so sure and questions his suitability for the task. "Ah, Sovereign LORD," he replies, "I do not know how to speak; I am only a child" (1:6). Even as Jeremiah addresses him as "Sovereign LORD," he questions God's will for him.

The Lord answers Jeremiah, taking his doubts seriously. God himself is to be his rescuer, and promises to remain with him. He need not be afraid of the people (1:8). Though Jeremiah had not raised the issue of fear, it was apparently at the root of his hesitation. As we'll see, given the details of how his life turned out, Jeremiah's fear of his countrymen was justified.

God makes it clear that obedience is not contrary to who Jeremiah is as a person. His call is even related to how Jeremiah was formed in his mother's womb. God had created him specifically to fulfill this calling. Then, Jeremiah is equipped for the task set before him, and God is the one who puts his words in the young prophet's mouth (1:7-10).

The Lord has Jeremiah begin in a very gentle way.

> The word of the LORD came to me: "What do you see, Jeremiah?"
>
> "I see the branch of an almond tree," I replied.
>
> The LORD said to me, "You have seen correctly, for I am watching to see that my word is fulfilled." (1:11-12)

Amazingly, this vision is for Jeremiah's benefit, to calm his fears and doubts, and to help him place his trust in the Lord. God emphasizes his faithfulness, using a play on words to make his point. In Hebrew, "almond branch" *(saqed)* sounds like "watching" *(soqed)*. God will be prompt in fulfilling his promises (as the almond is the first tree to blossom in the spring). God's presence and word, Jeremiah is assured, will not fail.

In the process of this conversation with the Lord, Jeremiah's perspective has been altered. Whereas before his concern was in his suitability and the people's response, now his thinking is centered on God's presence, power and Word.

It is at this point that Jeremiah's prophetic ministry begins (Jer 1:13). Now we can review Jeremiah's life and work, as it is recorded for us in the Scriptures. And as we do so, we will examine it with an eye toward the lessons we might learn concerning success and failure.

Snapshots from Jeremiah's Life

Before long the Lord returns with yet another promise. This one was far from reassuring: The people won't believe Jeremiah's message (7:27). Faithfulness, for this man, meant continuing in the face of knowing he would see no results. The people of his day met his proclamation of God's Word with undisguised hostility. Instead of repenting, they threatened to kill Jeremiah. So the Lord commanded his prophet to proclaim judgment against them (11:21-23)—which did little to resolve the conflict between Jeremiah and his protagonists.

Jeremiah's isolation deepened. There were other prophets around, but they were false—and God had him prophesy a special message of judgment against them (14:14-16). Harder still, even the comfort of marriage was kept from Jeremiah: "You must not marry," God told him, "and have sons or daughters in this place" (16:2).

Last night I spent an hour on the phone with a friend who

is a single woman. Gifted, intelligent, active, educated, a promising career—Sally seems to have everything going for her. Yet she cried as we talked together about relationships and marriage. She would like very much to be married—as would a growing number of single women in their thirties.[3] Now, after years of dating Christians, she had found a wonderful man—gentle, interesting, bright. He is also a non-Christian.

"Where are the Christian men worth considering?" Sally asked me. "And does it have to be either God or Jim?" At first she asked it as a rhetorical question, and I said nothing, knowing she knew the answer. But then she asked it again.

"Yes," I replied quietly, realizing she wanted to hear it aloud in the midst of the struggle. "Yes, it does. Your Lord has given you no choice."

I know what it is like to come home discouraged, to be with my wife who accepts and loves me. Marriage is a wondrous gift, and I cherish the escape from aloneness it affords me. Even those who embrace sexual freedom and scorn commitment yearn for the benefits only a family with continuity can provide.[4] Jeremiah was denied that. And that's a high price for faithfulness.

Jeremiah's opponents met together and planned their strategy for refuting his message (18:18). Increasingly, they showed up with prepared arguments and taunts to fling in his face. And still, they did not believe. Finally, violence erupted. Jeremiah was seized by Pashhur, the chief officer of the Temple, and beaten and restrained in stocks. There he sat, stared at by gawking crowds and tormented by swarms of flies while a numbing stiffness crept through his bruised and aching muscles (20:1-2). Even then, God didn't grant him respite. When Pashhur came to release him the next day, Jeremiah was commanded to prophesy disaster on him (20:3-6).

It's little wonder then that a great cry of anguish burst from Jeremiah before the Lord:

> O LORD, you deceived me, and I was deceived;
> you overpowered me and prevailed.
> I am ridiculed all day long;
> everyone mocks me.
> Whenever I speak, I cry out
> proclaiming violence and destruction.
> So the word of the LORD has brought me
> insult and reproach all day long.
> But if I say, "I will not mention him
> or speak any more in his name,"
> his word is in my heart like a fire,
> a fire shut up in my bones.
> I am weary of holding it in;
> indeed, I cannot.
> I hear many whispering,
> "Terror on every side! Report him! Let's report him!"
> All my friends are waiting for me to slip, saying,
> "Perhaps he will be deceived;
> then we will prevail over him and take our revenge on him." (20:7-10)

This is a cry of deep frustration from a man who knows what loneliness and disappointment are. The Scriptures record it as poetry, a work of poignant beauty that Jeremiah labored over as any artist would. But through the beauty, his pain is obvious. Jeremiah's life evidenced faithfulness, but are we prepared to call it successful?

Death threats continued, this time from the authorities, who demanded that Jeremiah be executed for the good of society and God (26:10-11). The threats could not be taken lightly. Another prophet named Uriah preached a message similar to Jeremiah's, and the king ordered his death. Uriah fled to Egypt, but the king's agents tracked him down and returned him to Judah, where the king had him killed (26:20-23). Once again, God instructs Jeremiah to preach judgment against his detractors. So they threw him into prison (32:3).

Then, at least for a moment, there was a hopeful sign. A scroll which Jeremiah had written was read to the king and his officials. This could have been the opening door to reform and national revival. Such things had happened before. On the other hand, it was dangerous to arouse royal displeasure. It was winter, and a fire had been lit to warm King Jehoiakim's feet. As the columns of the scroll were read, the king cut them off with a knife and arrogantly added them to the fire at his feet (36:21-24). Jeremiah's careful work was reduced to ashes. So the Lord had him rewrite the whole thing, adding a postscript of divine wrath against the king (36:27-31).

Unlike Uriah, Jeremiah outlived King Jehoiakim. He quickly fell foul of the next regime, however, and was accused of treason. The reasoning was interesting: The authorities reckoned that Jeremiah's warnings concerning sin were lowering the morale of the people, thus playing into the hands of their enemies. So they beat him yet again and threw him in a dungeon "where he remained a long time" (37:15-16). Later, he was transferred to a prison and kept on a diet of bread and water (37:21).

Then they came up with a more devious plan: "They took Jeremiah and put him into the cistern of Malkijah, the king's son, which was in the courtyard of the guard. They lowered Jeremiah by ropes into the cistern; it had no water in it, only mud, and Jeremiah sank down into the mud" (38:6).

It seems to me there is a great deal of understatement in this report. How rough were they as they lowered him into the darkness? Did they know there was no water? Did they care? We also don't know how long he remained there or how weakened his condition was. Nor do we know how deep the mud was. Did Jeremiah struggle? We are told that an official intervened before he starved, sending him back to prison (38:7-13). And still Jeremiah told them God's word, still the people didn't believe, still he saw no results.

The Scriptures do not tell how Jeremiah died, though we do know he was taken to Egypt against his will (43:6-7). One tradition says he escaped from there and made his way to Babylon, where he later died. Another tradition has it that he was finally silenced by being stoned to death in Egypt.[5] In any case, it's little wonder that Jeremiah described himself as "the man who has seen affliction" (Lam 3:1).

What Failure? What Success?

Jeremiah was tenacious, no doubt about it. Courageous too. But how should we think about him in relation to success and failure?

Was Jeremiah a success? I wouldn't wish to be on record as calling him a failure. He was a prophet of the Most High God. Though the kings of his era are largely forgotten, his writings have survived the ages as part of God's revealed Word. His insistence on truth was unwavering in the face of unbelief. His stand against evil was informed not by immediate results, but by the holiness of God. In the face of mood swings, poverty, torture and the frustration of seeing his society reject truth for lies, his faithfulness to God was firm. Surely this is not failure.

But how do we account for the poverty and lack of results?

Are these the measure of his success? A biblically informed response is no.

To suggest that Jeremiah was a success because he was poor, or that the prophet Samuel was less spiritual because he never had to endure such deprivation, are conclusions that find no support in the Scriptures. Jeremiah didn't garner a multitude of converts, but was that his fault? And was that his purpose? Jeremiah did not enjoy the public respect that Moses did, but is human esteem the standard of goodness? Jeremiah did not experience the wealth of Abraham, but is the purpose of life rooted in material things?

Jeremiah was faithful before the Lord, and that is the essence of success. In his faithfulness Jeremiah pleased God.

Jeremiah's courageous walk of faith is beyond my experience. How could he continue to warn the people when he was so shabbily treated? What was the point? If the people will not listen to reason, then be done with them. Let them be damned—they deserve it! Or so goes my faithless thinking.

When I read Jeremiah's story, I find myself questioning God's goodness. Remember the promise God had made? "Do not be afraid of them, for I am with you and will rescue you" (Jer 1:8), the Lord had assured him. Did God fulfill that promise? Do we see any evidence of it? The answer was apparently clear to Jeremiah:

> Because of the LORD's great love we are not consumed,
> for his compassions never fail.
>
> They are new every morning;
> great is your faithfulness. (Lam 3:22-23)

In the midst of repression and frustration and deprivation, Jeremiah experienced God's trustworthiness. Apparently Jeremiah did not doubt that God had fulfilled his promise.

This should alert us to the danger of interpreting God's promises by our standards of success, ease and prosperity. Many of us assume that if we're faithful to him, then God really owes us at least a comfortable standard of living. Isn't that what "meet all your needs" (Phil 4:19) means? Then again, we probably thought we knew what "rescue" would mean when God promised to be with Jeremiah. In fact, it did not always mean that he would be spared harm. His life ought to warn us against assuming we know what a successful Christian life may consist of.

Jeremiah was successful before God in the *midst* of hard times, not because of them. We see that success measured as wealth, power, fame, self-fulfillment or appearance is clearly inadequate in light of Jeremiah's life. Jeremiah's success is found in his faithfulness, not in his circumstances.

Hebrews 11: A Sudden Shift

Hebrews 11 is a chapter of heroes—biblical success stories, if you will. It is also a chapter of sinners. David is here, the one who murdered a man in an attempt to cover up the sexual adventure he had had with that man's wife. Samson is listed too, who is as famous for his loose life as for his godly exploits. And Rahab, the prostitute, who lied to save the Israelite spies. These are listed here not because they were perfect, but because they lived by faith. They trusted God; they were faithful.

Living by faith is at the heart of what is most revolutionary about Christianity. It alone points the way to life in the midst of death, to stability and freedom when all around is the slippery nonsense of relativism.

Living by faith means trusting the God who has proven himself to be trustworthy. That requires knowing him personally, not just knowing about him.[6] *Living by faith means living moment by moment as if God exists and as if his Word is true.* It means a life of faithfulness before the God who is there.

The people listed in Hebrews 11 did just that. They were not superheroes like the comic figures in Saturday morning cartoons. They were people like us. As we read the details of their lives we can take heart that we aren't of such poor stock that there is no hope for us. These are people who are on record as having lived by faith: "[Faith] is what the ancients were commended for" (Heb 11:2). Commended by whom? By God himself. And that is a weighty measure of success.

So the carefully constructed list begins: Adam, Abel, Enoch, Noah, Abraham, Sarah . . . (11:4-31). But now read the list with our society's definition of success in mind. Some, like Sarah and Abraham, experienced great wealth in their lifetime. Others, like Joseph, had great authority; he was second only to Pharaoh at a time when Egypt was a world power. Moses was granted fame, a reputation that remains to this day. Isn't it possible that some of these might be considered successful if they lived today? Others listed here, on the other hand, might be laughed at, as Noah was in his own day, or locked quietly away in a back ward.

"What More Shall I Say?"

Then we come to a break in the narrative. Until verse 31, the author has been moving through Israel's history chronologically and has come to the conquest of Jericho. Then the writer breaks off the annotated list and speeds up the pace.

> And what more shall I say? I do not have time to tell about Gideon, Barak, Samson, Jephthah, David, Samuel and the prophets, who through faith conquered kingdoms, administered justice, and gained what was promised; who shut the

> mouths of lions, quenched the fury of the flames, and escaped the edge of the sword; whose weakness was turned to strength; and who became powerful in battle and routed foreign armies. Women received back their dead, raised to life again. Others were tortured and refused to be released, so that they might gain a better resurrection. Some faced jeers and flogging, while still others were chained and put in prison. They were stoned; they were sawed in two; they were put to death by the sword. They went about in sheepskins and goatskins, destitute, persecuted and mistreated—the world was not worthy of them. They wandered in deserts and mountains, and in caves and holes in the ground. These were all commended for their faith. (11:32-39)

What can we learn from this passage for our study? First, a simple observation: the list concerns people who were commended by God for their faith in him and his Word. The author has not changed topics in this second half of the chapter.

Second, being faithful sometimes results in spectacular achievements. Routing armies, resurrections, escaping death, bringing justice—without doubt these people would be featured in glossy magazines. Some of these results could be easily considered successes even by our secular society's measures. But this passage insists on more than that.

Sometimes faithfulness results in seeming failure: being stoned to death, destitute, homeless, tortured, even sawed in half. All are part of the same list. These misfortunes also came to those who were "commended for their faith." Of course, some of these might appear in glossy magazines too, but probably not in an article on success or on pleasing God.

Hebrews 11 clearly exposes the deficiency of the Gospel of Prosperity. If anyone had "Cadillac faith," these people did. Yet only some of them experienced "Cadillac" circumstances. It is unbiblical to maintain that those who have faith will always receive the material benefits of success.

Similarly, this passage exposes the deficiency of the Gospel of Simple Living. Wealth, fame, power, self-fulfillment and appearance are not evil, per se. It's unbiblical to believe that faithful believers will never be granted such things. In fact they can come to godly people, and others, equally commended by God, can remain in obscurity and deprivation. What is important for both groups of people is their faithfulness.

Exercising faith in God is not merely subjective, though it does involve our emotions. For the faithful mentioned in Hebrews 11, things changed as a result of their believing God. If they had not believed, events would have turned out differently for them—and for history. But their faithfulness didn't guarantee heroic accomplishments or escape from negative circumstances.

Like Jeremiah and those of Hebrews 11, we are called to faithfulness, to living as though God exists and as though his Word is true. Compared to this standard, today's success, as well as the usual Christian versions, are inadequate.

Solomon: The Seduction of Idolatry
Solomon lived about three hundred fifty years before Jeremiah. More than any other king, he represents the full flowering of the Israelite monarchy. "What Solomon became," historian Paul Johnson says, "was a Near Eastern monarch of outstanding skill."[7] In contrast to his father David's reign, Solomon ruled during a period of peace, when the large militaristic empires surrounding Palestine tended to be quiet. David had been occupied with the consolidation of the kingdom. Solomon could

turn his attention to economic, judicial and cultural matters.

The transfer of power after David's death was not without incident, but in a short time Solomon had purged the usurpers and established his right to the throne (1 Kings 1—2). Early in his career the Lord appeared to Solomon in a dream, inviting him to ask for whatever he desired. Making a godly choice, he requested wisdom. The Lord was pleased and gave him great wealth, honor and fame as well (3:10-14).

We don't know the extent of Solomon's wisdom, but his reign was so marked with discernment that his subjects were in awe of him (3:28). He was known as a man whose wisdom "was greater than the wisdom of all the men of the East, and greater than all the wisdom of Egypt" (4:30). His fame spread throughout the known world (4:31), and one neighboring monarch traveled over twelve hundred miles to see for herself whether the stories were true (1 Kings 10).

Solomon was a poet and songwriter, composing over a thousand musical pieces (4:32), as well as his famous love poem, the Song of Songs. He was a man of science, involved with the taxonomy of both plants and animals (4:33). Solomon's court turned into a lecture hall when kings sent representatives to learn from him (4:34).

Due to its unique geographical position in the ancient world, Israel was able to prosper economically during peace times and with wise administration.[8] The use of the camel had opened up trade, and the Israelite monarch was able to control the trade routes from Egypt and Arabia to the Fertile Crescent. As part of this effort, Solomon built an oasis called Palmyra, or Tadmor, about a hundred forty miles northeast of Damascus (9:18). He reorganized the nation to further economic development, levied taxes (4:7-19), built up smelting and trade in iron and copper, and became a middleman in the lucrative business of horse- and chariot-trading (10:28-29).

Solomon was adept at foreign affairs, making treaties and cultivating royal marriages (3:1). When the time came to build the Temple in Jerusalem, he was easily able to get the lumber he needed from Hiram, king of Tyre (1 Kings 5). The construction of the Temple was the project David his father had dreamed of, but had not been allowed to realize. The splendor and artistry involved made the finished product an architectural accomplishment to rival the great buildings of antiquity (1 Kings 6—7). The songs of praise and the prayer of dedication delivered by King Solomon at the opening rightly take their place in the classic liturgical literature of all time (1 Kings 8:23-53).

Over the years Solomon married many times, often to women from pagan backgrounds and cultures. They brought their false gods into his harem, and Solomon began to adopt the values and myths of these idols and to worship them (1 Kings 11:4-13). By the end of his life, the Scriptures record, "his heart was not fully devoted to the Lord his God." Because of his place of leadership, the results of this sin naturally flowed out to affect the entire nation. Though he started his reign in great promise, Solomon's final days were marred with dishonor. The moral, religious and judicial decline set in motion by Solomon's apostasy was to mark Israel for the next three-and-a-half centuries. The process of decadence that began with Solomon came to fruition in Jeremiah's day. The nation, by then shot through with idolatry, underwent the wrath of a holy God.

From Success to Failure
What can we take from this study of Solomon's life to shed light on our understanding of success and failure? What principles

can we glean that are applicable to our thinking and lives?

Was Solomon a success? He certainly comes closer to our society's notion of success than Jeremiah ever did. But is that a sufficient analysis for the Christian? Wouldn't it be more accurate to say he reached the heights of God's blessing and success, only to choose to descend into moral, intellectual and spiritual failure?

What about Solomon's wealth and fame? Were these the essence of his success, or the ultimate cause of his failure? The answer is clearly no. Solomon's wealth and fame, along with his wisdom, were good gifts of God over which he was to exercise a stewardly care. They could be used for God's glory, or debased to honor the likes of Molech and Baal. Wealth, power and fame were not his success, nor were they his failure. Solomon began well and ended poorly not because of wealth and fame, but in the midst of them. The heart of the problem was his lack of faithfulness to God and to his Word.

Once again the Gospels of Prosperity and Simple Living are called into question. Solomon remained wealthy and powerful until his dying day, but his final years were not pleasing to God (contra Prosperity). And his failure was not linked to his having accumulated wealth (contra Simple Living).

Wealth and poverty, fame and obscurity, power and helplessness, fulfillment and boredom—these are not the essence of life, nor of spirituality. They do not speak to success or failure. We are to be faithful before God, living a life marked by trust, in the midst of whatever circumstances he has ordained for us. The important issue is not the nature of our circumstances but whether we are pleasing God.

Being captive to a materialistic world view is grievous for Christians but unsurprising. It can express itself either by glorifying poverty or glorifying wealth. That the two sides war with one another must not blind us to their similar roots.

Solomon's real success or failure cannot be measured by his wealth, power or fame. Faithfulness or lack of faith: that is the crucial issue.

Redefining Success
How, then, are we to understand success? What can we learn from Jeremiah, from the list of the faithful in Hebrews 11 and from Solomon?

From Jeremiah we learn that, for the Christian, success is not defined by measurable results or cultural acclaim. Jeremiah saw neither yet pleased God. Though no one believed, and he had to watch his people suppress God's truth and invite his wrath, yet this man was no failure.

We learn from Hebrews 11 that both positive and negative results can flow into the lives of those who please God. One who is faithful before God might achieve wonderful things or might experience an unbelievable amount of suffering.

Solomon's example teaches us that the culture's assessment of someone might be dead wrong. Certainly our society would see Solomon as a success. Who cares if he became religiously pluralistic in his old age? But whether people applaud or not, Solomon's faithlessness was his failure and his undoing.

Wealth, power, fame, self-fulfillment and appearance do not in themselves signal either success or failure. The Scriptures record virtually every possible combination. Abraham and Sarah were wealthy, and they pleased God. Jeremiah was desperately poor but no failure. Lot and Solomon were wealthy, yet ended their lives in dishonor. Daniel occupied a position of enormous power and was "highly esteemed" by God (Dan

10:19). King Ahab abused his authority as all statists do and was rightly denounced by the prophet. Moses had great fame, yet most believers are remembered only by God. Esther faced great stresses and struggles, but the results of her efforts must have been deeply fulfilling. Jonah, on the other hand, seemed more frustrated than fulfilled.

Our definition of success must be rooted ultimately in what pleases God. Being crowned a success by man but declared a failure by God is hardly a notable achievement. Jesus referred to such a person as a fool (Lk 12:20). If our lives are centered in him alone, then our perspective on success must resonate with his pleasure. "Man's chief end," the Westminster Confession reminds us, "is to glorify God, and to enjoy him forever."

A practical understanding of success for the Christian must comprise faithfulness to God and to his Word. "Without faith," we are told, "it is impossible to please God" (Heb 11:6). Our life is either built around God and his word, or it is built around something else. Finally, life is a matter of worship. We either worship idols, or the true God. Either the God and Father of our Lord Jesus Christ is our reference point for life, or we have given his honor to another.

But what does pleasing God consist of? What does faithfulness mean for Christians in the closing years of the twentieth century? The struggle to live in faith today is the subject we will turn to next.

Questions for Individuals and Groups

1. Explore more fully the stories of Solomon, Jeremiah and those listed in Hebrews 11. Which do you identify with most? Why? (You might find it helpful to use a concordance and Bible dictionary.)

2. Many single Christians feel like failures because they have not married. How does the church contribute to this?

How should singles feel?

3. Finding signs of cultural success in people's lives is relatively easy. They either have wealth, fame, power, self-fulfillment or appearance—or they don't. How can we identify faithfulness in each other?

4. In what ways does your understanding of faithfulness before God conflict with the demands of your career? your family? your friends?

What struggles and problems result from this? What plans should you make to deal with these conflicts?

5. How would your view of success and failure explain the sort of experience Elisabeth Elliot had to undergo? What if your whole life was a string of tragedies?

6. In what ways could financial bankruptcy be a symptom of sin or unfaithfulness in a Christian's life?

Could it ever come in the midst of real faithfulness? What would it signal then?

7. Imagine that you are a journalist for a glossy magazine. How might you report some of the stories listed in Hebrews 11?

Too often we have made Christianity into a happiness system, guaranteeing success the easy way, with God there in his power to fill in the gaps.
Hans Rookmaaker

Annie: "Alvy, you're incapable of enjoying life, you know that?"
Alvy: "I can't enjoy anything unless . . . everyone is . . . you know, if one guy is starving someplace . . . it puts a crimp in my evening."
From the movie "Annie Hall" by Woody Allen

For faith does not certainly promise itself either length of years or honor or riches in this life, since the Lord willed that none of these things be appointed for us. But it is content with this certainty: that, however many things fail us that have to do with the maintenance of this life, God will never fail.
John Calvin

If, drunk with sight of power, we loose
Wild tongues that have not Thee in awe,
Such boastings as the Gentiles use,
Or lesser breeds without the Law.
Rudyard Kipling

CHAPTER 6

HOW GOD USES THE WORLD'S SUCCESS

It just wasn't right. King Tiglath-pileser III—Pul, for short—was riding high while the people of God struggled to make ends meet.[1]

Pul had arrived abruptly on the Assyrian scene. He wasn't from a royal family, but was either a general or province governor (his background is unclear)—and was suddenly made king of Assyria. And his appointment went undisputed. Usually new kings had trouble on their hands, beating back rivals who wanted the crown themselves. But apparently Pul wasn't a man to be trifled with.

And that was just the beginning. Pul mustered the Assyrian army and began to march, first south into Babylon, and then west into Syria and Israel. None could stand before him, and the tribute he extracted from the conquered lands was immense. Wealth flowed into the nation, and soon Assyria stood at the center of the known world.

Previous kings had faced endless difficulties ruling empires with far-flung provinces. The people were sure to give tribute when the army was there threatening them with destruction. But when the armies returned to the mother province, rebellions were the order of the day.

Pul solved that problem with an innovation that tied his empire together. Wherever Pul went, he uprooted the best of the populace and forced them to migrate to a far corner of his domain. Masses of people were marched in criss-cross patterns from Palestine to Mesopotamia. The results were stunning, at least from an imperial viewpoint. Rebellion decreased because it was harder for strangers to unify. Local economies were disrupted, and people had to struggle simply to stay alive. Soon the Assyrian empire stretched from the Mediterranean Sea into Asia. Pul was sitting on a mountain of power and wealth and fame in the palace in Nineveh.

But from the Jewish perspective, this just wasn't right. Pul was an evil king who had never honored God. Assyria was cruel and militaristic, a pagan culture riddled with idolatry. And Israel was one of those provinces being sucked dry by the ruinous tribute Pul so gleefully collected. It's true that Israel had turned away from God and his Word, but they were still the covenant people of God. "We are yours from of old," Isaiah complained to God, "but you have not ruled over them, they have not been called by your name" (Is 63:19). Once so prosperous and free, the nation of Israel now saw the treasures of their land stripped away by unclean hands. It just wasn't right that Assyria should be so successful, so powerful, so prosperous and Israel so deprived, so divided, so poor. How could such an anomaly fit into God's plan?

Success and the Plan of God

Today we wrestle with the same questions of the meaning of success and failure, dressed in the details of our own lives. The stories of Jeremiah, Moses, Daniel and others only underscore the same issues. How does God view earthly success and failure in his people's lives? How does he, in his sovereignty, use these for his glory? How do today's measures of success figure in God's redemptive plan in history?

Although we've seen that wealth, power, fame, self-fulfillment and appearance are an insufficient definition of success for Christians, we can't live as if they never affect us, because they do. All of us experience some measure of success or failure as the world counts such things. And we feel the pressure to conform from parents, friends or supervisors. According to our circumstances, we are all stewards of the money, authority, popularity and satisfaction in life we've received. Or perhaps we struggle with their absence.

This brings us back to the issues raised by the prophet Isaiah. What is the biblical perspective? How do money and power fit in redemptive history and in our lives? If we are successful, what does God expect of us? And if we have failed, what is his response? What does it mean to see the elements of success as God does? If we're to live faithfully in the midst of the success society, we'll need to find these answers.

It is deadly to regard the trappings of success as the measure of an individual's worth. Such a view reduces a person to the value of things destined to perish. The extent of the Fall is evident when creatures made in God's image actually believe their significance is linked to the fluctuations of the stock market or the fickle opinions of society.

God remains active in his creation, bringing history to its biblical consummation. Coming to understand where wealth, fame, power and self-fulfillment and appearance fit in his plan will cause us to respond to them—or their absence—in a manner befitting the people of God.

From God's perspective, wealth, fame and the rest can be seen as:

1. the blessing of God
2. the testing of God
3. the temptation of the enemy or
4. the judgment of God

These four possibilities aren't mutually exclusive. What God grants as blessing can be used by the enemy to tempt us to sin. God's blessing always tests the affection of our hearts, and if we concentrate on the blessing instead of the Blesser, we may discover that the blessing has become a crushing weight of judgment.

The Blessing of God

The world's measure of success can be legitimate blessings from God, gifts given to be used for his glory. The Old Testament people of God knew the Lord was the source of their income and prosperity (Deut 8:18). Abraham was given great wealth, and his descendants were promised the land—the primary form of capital in that day (Gen 13:15). The apostle Paul could speak of "glory" and "good report" in his life and work (2 Cor 6:8). The early Christians exhibited such spiritual power that their contemporaries spoke of them as having turned the world upside down (Acts 17:6). And Jesus spoke with such power and authority that his hearers were amazed (Mk 1:27).

The New Testament people of God are taught that God is the source of income. Paul instructed Timothy to teach "those who are rich" to trust God "who richly provides us with everything for our enjoyment" (1 Tim 6:17). The Bible is consistent in its emphasis that it is to God alone that we must look for sustenance (Ps 104:14-15; Mt 6:11, 33). The Puritan Cotton Mather had it correct when he said, "In our occupations we spread our nets; but it is God who brings unto our nets all that comes into them."[2] This is why the Scriptures are so insistent that we be filled with thanksgiving for what we receive (Col 3:15; 1 Thess 5:18).

And we may look at our own experience of God's provision and grace to see that these blessings can come as an expression of his goodness to us. In the early years of our marriage, my wife and I foolishly went into debt to purchase a car. It was an impulsive choice, uninformed by prayer, and we soon came to regret it. The car was a lemon, and repair bills piled up until that automobile seemed to us to be God's way to teach us a hard lesson in managing finances.

Finally the car was paid off, and the time came to get another vehicle. We found a car we liked, but this time we determined to wait on the Lord. The day before our decision had to be made, a friend who knew nothing of our problem stopped me in the car park at church. "Our kids are off at college," he told me. "We don't need three vehicles, so you can have one. I'd like to give it to you." I was stunned, but grateful to both him and to the Lord. This was the grace of God! That car met our financial need, and to us, at least, it had "Blessing of your heavenly Father" written all over it. We knew our loving Father's hand had been at work; even though acquiring automobiles free of charge certainly hasn't been the norm for us.

In terms of fame, there are some—John Stott, Charles Colson, Aleksandr Solzhenitsyn and Elisabeth Elliot come quickly to mind—whose high reputation as Christian leaders has been used to expand their witness to the truth. God told Joshua that he would "exalt" him, increasing his fame among all the people (Josh 3:7). Clearly, fame can have all the hallmarks of God's blessing.

Years ago I had the pleasure of working for a godly man. Jim exercised authority as my supervisor, a form of power that was never abused. But he took that power seriously and was a leader who expected me to learn to follow. More than a few times he stepped in to change my plans. Although he was eager to talk it all through in detail, when push came to shove, he was the boss. Long before the Lord took him home suddenly in a road accident, I realized how much I appreciated his leadership. He had helped me set balanced priorities, encouraged my growth and helped me face areas where I needed to change. This was an example to me of power used to glorify God. Jim was not afraid to embrace the authority that he had been given, and therefore his ministry to me in my life and work was profound.

Even self-fulfillment is not necessarily contrary to the good blessing of God. When Jesus acted in obedience at the well in Samaria he experienced a euphoria so real that even the need for food and drink seemed to fade (Jn 4:31-34). Faithfulness to his Father was deeply fulfilling to him.

Isn't it also possible to experience deep satisfaction in the midst of our work? The psalmist, in giving thanks for the graciousness of the Lord, includes man's labor in his list of good gifts (Ps 104:23). In the midst of slogging through life, it can be a wondrous thing to experience deep fulfillment in our work.

Sometimes, at least for a brief period, we can be so involved and enveloped in a project that we seem to lose ourselves, and time ceases to be an issue. These periods of human fulfillment are the blessing of God, and to hold them suspect is to risk blasphemy.

The Proper Use of Blessings

To be given a measure of wealth, fame, power and self-fulfillment is to be given a gift to be used with great care for the glory of God. Jesus' story of the talents (Mt 25:14-30) illustrates the proper approach to such stewardship. Servants were each given talents, and the responsibility to invest them wisely. The talents were not to be treated carelessly, nor were they to be despised. When the master returned, he expected a net increase when the books were balanced. And those who had used their talents wisely were those who pleased the master.

History records numerous examples of believers who wisely invested their blessings. William Wilberforce, a Member of Parliament, exercised political power for the Lord.[3] He labored tirelessly to end slavery in Britain and readily used his position of influence to fight for justice. Wilberforce sought power and learned to use it judiciously. On the night that the vote finally took place, Wilberforce turned in joy to his friend Henry Thornton: "Well, Henry. What do we abolish next?" This is a godly use of power as a blessing, and a godly enjoyment of that blessing as well. The good gifts of God can be used to his honor or squandered on lesser things. The choice lies with the steward.

An Unjust Blessing?

Some might object at this point, arguing that in the modern

world, Western wealth is the result of an unjust economic system. While Abraham's wealth may have come as God's blessing, that kind of blessing couldn't be godly today. In fact, mere involvement in the free enterprise system may involve us in systematic injustice.[4] "The people of the nonindustrialized world are poor because we are rich; the poverty of the masses is maintained and perpetuated by our systems and institutions and by the way we live our lives."[5]

This is a serious charge. For Christians, neither the way we gain our income nor the way we use it can be contrary to godliness. We must strive to be scrupulously honest in all the details of our work—but what if we discover that our company is a cover for an extortion racket? The human race remains fallen. Financial sin and economic exploitation is real and can occur at all levels of the marketplace. Christians must speak out forcefully against injustice and work hard to stop it wherever it occurs.[6]

But the real culprit is not freedom in the market, it is sin in the human heart. Freedom is a gift of God, though enjoyed by relatively few. Too many are eager to dispense with freedom in order to implement a particular view of the politically just society.[7]

Christian economist Brian Griffiths notes: "I believe that it is entirely false to suggest that the wealth of the West is at present being obtained at the expense of Third World countries or that the poverty of the Third World is the result of systematic exploitation by the West."[8] A market economy can provide "an enormous opportunity for Christians in business to create structures at work which are authentically Christian."[9]

Certainly, wealth can be increased without exploitation. As people add creativity and hard work to the resources available in God's creation, what they produce has an increased value or usefulness. This is the creation of wealth.[10] Farmers plant seed, working the soil, cultivating the plants and producing a harvest. An artist takes pigments, a brush and palette, and applies his skill to a canvas—and the assorted dabs of paint are transformed into a valuable work of art. The creation of wealth can simultaneously serve mankind and glorify the Lord.

Of course, not all economic systems allow for such development. Indeed, a "market economy with a widely dispersed ownership of property and capital is a far more effective way of creating wealth than state ownership or state control."[11] It is true that materialism, corruption and greed are the opposite of godliness. But these things are not intrinsic to the business sphere any more than pornography is intrinsic to photography. The church must encourage those who are gifted in the creation of wealth to pursue their calling to the glory of God, and not abandon it. Using these gifts can expand employment, so that increasing numbers of families can be rescued from the curse of joblessness. This gift must be prayerfully developed in the midst of giving sacrificially, and working to preserve freedom and end injustice.

Wealth, power, fame and self-fulfillment are mistakenly used by our culture as the final measures of success. But they can be the blessing of God, and must be treated as carefully as any of God's good gifts. However, potent gifts must also be handled with the recognition that they can come as the testing of God.

The Testing of God

Perhaps, in this fallen world, it is safest to assume that God's gifts are both his blessing and his testing simultaneously. Life moment by moment involves choice: "Choose for yourselves this day whom you will serve" (Josh 24:15). What God blesses us with can be used to test our faith in him, and our eagerness to abide in him alone. "We are not trying to please men but God," writes the apostle, "who tests our hearts" (1 Thess 2:4). David, who would have qualified as a success in our society, could declare: "I know, my God, that you test the heart and are pleased with integrity" (1 Chron 29:17).

In 725 B.C. in Judah, Isaiah was prophet and Hezekiah was king. Hezekiah is remembered as a godly reformer who worked hard to remove the idols that dotted the countryside. He worked to strengthen the nation so that their servitude to the Assyrian king might end. The Scripture records that the Lord blessed Hezekiah with "very great riches and honor" (2 Chron 32:27-30). Later, this blessing became a test.

Near the end of Hezekiah's life, diplomats came to visit him from Babylon. The king had just recovered from a fatal illness. It was at this moment that "God left him to test him and to know everything that was in his heart" (2 Chron 32:31). Unfortunately, Hezekiah failed miserably. In an egotistical flaunting of his power and wealth, the king foolishly paraded the treasures of Israel before his eager visitors. Babylon, with its growing military might, was on the lookout for easy pickings. The prophet Isaiah was sent to Hezekiah with the news that as a result of this indiscretion, the nation would be plundered. The very things that God had blessed Hezekiah with became his stumbling block. And when he fell, he took an entire nation with him. The testing of God is a serious business, indeed.

Illustrations of how God can use success to test his creatures are easy to find in history. George Müller was blessed with substantial sums of money. Over the course of a lifetime he ministered to thousands of destitute children.[12] The need to care for orphans was great, and he responded, calling the church to social action, prayer and a demonstration of love. Müller consciously saw the money that came to him as both a blessing and a test. He struggled throughout his life to not place his trust in fund-raising techniques or in wealthy benefactors, but in the Lord alone. He carefully ordered his life and ministry along stringent principles designed to keep his eyes on the Lord. Each gift not only met the needs of orphans but stretched Müller's faith, and served to test his reliance on the God who had called him into service.

To be tested by God is something we should expect. Though the testing that comes to us might be very different from Hezekiah's and Müller's, the basic principle remains the same. There are many ways we might be tested, and the cultural standards of success might be included as part of the examination sent our way. How we handle wealth, power, fame and self-fulfillment and appearance—or their absence—all put our integrity on the line. With or without them, the mandate of faithfulness remains the same. If we make these things the center of our affections instead of God, then whether we have them or only dream of them is unimportant. An idolater who is poor is as condemned as one who is rich.

As long as these perks of cultural success are ours, we must handle them with great care. They can be the wedge that turns our hearts from our Lord. Prudence suggests a constant vigilance. It is worth our while not to fail, for it is in the midst of testing that faithfulness is purified like fine gold.

The Temptation of the Enemy
Wealth, power, fame, self-fulfillment and appearance can be blessings from the Father, or they can be used to test us. But

there is also the chance that the Enemy will tempt us with them. Success is a powerful enticement, and Satan's tendency to appear as an angel of light can mask the danger. Fiery darts fly fast, and our opponent is learned in the techniques of ambush.

Learning to recognize temptation and gaining skill in the use of divine armor is part of Christian discipleship.[13] Succumbing to the Tempter's whispered half-truths is not only a constant danger, it can be a discouraging reality—especially if our folly seems to be a weary repeat of past failures. All Christians share the shame of saying yes to temptation. The poet John Donne knew something of this struggle. And, as a Christian, he also knew the only adequate solution: the grace of God.

> Wilt thou forgive that sinne where I begunne,
> Which was my sin, though it were done before?
> Wilt thou forgive that sinne; through which I runne,
> And do run still: though still I do deplore?
> When thou hast done, thou hast not done,
> For, I have more.
>
> Wilt thou forgive that sinne which I have wonne
> Others to sinne? and, made my sinne their doore?
> Wilt thou forgive that sinne which I did shunne
> A yeare, or two: but wallowed in, a score?
> When thou hast done, thou hast not done,
> For, I have more.
>
> I have a sinne of feare, that when I have spunne
> My last thread, I shall perish on the shore;
> But sweare by thy selfe, that at my death thy sonne
> Shall shine as he shines now, and heretofore;

>   And having done that, Thou hast done,
>   I feare no more.[14]

If the love of money is the root of all kinds of evil (1 Tim 6:10), then it is likely that where there is wealth, the Enemy will be lurking close by. Since power can be so easily corrupted to oppress instead of heal, we should be prepared for attack. Self-fulfillment and fame can quickly lead to selfishness and pride, rather than being used as gifts for God's glory.

The temptations that Jesus endured for us involved similar enticements (Lk 4:1-13). A series of crafty snares were set by Satan. But Jesus, though tempted with power and riches and fame, remained faithful to his Father.

Jesus warned his followers about these temptations in the parable of the four soils. There are those who hear the Word, but like seed planted alongside thorns, "the worries of this life, the deceitfulness of wealth and the desires for other things" choke off its life (Mk 4:19). Any fruitfulness there might have been withers fast.

When David was king, Satan enticed him into taking a census of Israel, which was for David a sin (1 Chron 21:1; also note 2 Sam 24). The rebellion in that act may not be obvious to us, but rebellion it was. One of the most likely reasons a Middle Eastern king of that time would order a census was to muster troops for battle. When David told Joab to number the people, Joab found the king's command "repulsive," and advised against doing it (1 Chron 21:3, 6). But David's mind was made up, and the census went forward.

God had established Israel as a nation, and had promised that their enemies would be his enemies. He had already proven that numbers weren't the primary factor in the outcome of battles. Gideon had been limited to three hundred men but had defeated the Mideanites. And Joshua's superior force had been beaten back by the little town of Ai. God wanted his people to trust him. If he was present and fighting, no enemy—regardless of the odds—could stand before Israel.

David's census flew in the face of that trust. Under pressure from the Philistines, David succumbed to the Tempter's suggestion that he set aside faithfulness in order to act like a king. Numbering the people would allow him to identify his resources and make plans for war. What he should have been doing was waiting on the Lord. Satan tempted David with an abuse of power, and the results were painful (1 Chron 21:11-19).

The challenge is to learn to sense the spiritual danger in the trappings of success before we become ensnared. No matter how deeply we love our Lord, success can easily seduce us. Despite the details of our sin, the bottom line is still death. Whether we are tempted by pride, thievery, covetousness or the abuse of others is not the crucial point. In each case, what we have done in listening to the Tempter is to engage in spiritual promiscuity. Success or failure can be a quiet time-bomb delivered personally by the enemy of our souls.

The Judgment of God

Judgment is another way that God can use wealth, power, fame, self-fulfillment and appearance in our lives. But, as Charles Colson points out, we might not even recognize God's wrath if it were poured out on our own society:

> Could it be that judgment is already upon us? Instead of balls of fire hurled down from above or visitations of plagues and boils, perhaps God is simply allowing us to wallow helplessly in the mire of our sin. Augustine's statement, "The punishment of sin is sin," captures the essence of this kind of judg-

ment. . . . The message is clear: if we insist on continuing to eat forbidden fruit, then we will be allowed to glut ourselves with it until we retch and vomit—or until our stomachs burst. Sin leads to certain destruction. It is the most fearsome form of judgment.[15]

The very things that can be precious gifts can also be burning coals heaped up to consume the unrighteous. This is true for an individual as well as for an entire culture. Read again of Absalom's thirst for power and how it destroyed him (2 Sam 14—18) or of Judas's pathetic desire for a bit of silver that led not just to death but to damnation (Mt 27:1-10). Success can destroy and kill.

The judgment which Paul says is presently being revealed from heaven (Rom 1:18-32) is not the abrupt intervention of divine wrath that was evidenced with Korah and his comrades in rebellion when the ground opened to swallow them up (Num 16). Rather, Paul describes here the inexorable process where human beings are slowly strangled by their own wickedness. Three times he stresses that "God gave them over" to their sinfulness (Rom 1:24, 26, 28). The process is not one "of exterior censure, but by a rotting from within. The lustful and depraved are given over completely to their own passions."[16]

The fact that this form of judgment is less dramatic than chasms suddenly opening to swallow the rebels must not blind us to its horror. Either way, it is a fearful thing to be a sinner in the hands of an angry God (Heb 10:31).

It is better to have locusts or famine than the sentence of being gradually swallowed up unawares in the cesspool of our own greed and lust and hate. To starve to death has some degree of dignity—it is the result of exterior forces. But to die a slow and dull-eyed death of excess, even as we cram more sweets into our drooling mouths, is the ultimate debasement.[17]

Colson correctly suggests that this might be what is happening in the West as the twentieth century draws to a close. The measures of success can be used in this ongoing expression of God's wrath on a sinful world. Success and failure can be used by a sovereign God to reprove wickedness and show his righteousness.

After David had taken the census, the prophet Gad was sent to the king with the message of divine wrath (1 Chron 21:9-13). It's almost as if God were saying, "Okay, big shot. You want to act like a king, do you? All right, here's a decision for you: make a choice. Isn't making decisions a king-like thing to do?" But the choice was one of horror. There would be three years of famine or three months of being defeated by enemies or three days when the sword of the Lord would be unleashed in the land. In the end, seventy thousand perished. So much for being so concerned about numbers. David's power was turned against himself as God's holy judgment against his faithlessness.

To respond to success Christianly means we must not be tricked into wearing spectacles which only see the here and now. Around us rages the spiritual battle. And part of the onslaught is the seduction of Success, softly beckoning to the unwary.

Contentment

As we've seen, the world's measures of success, evaluated from the perspective of God's plan in history, fall into four possible categories. They can be God's blessing, but they can also be his testing. The Enemy can use them to entice us to faithlessness. Or they can become a vehicle of God's wrath and judgment on those who have spurned his truth and accepted a lie.

The Lord has promised to return soon. Until then, we are to be faithful. That means faithfulness with wealth, fame, power, self-fulfillment and appearance—or without them.

The world's measures of success must never be seen as the essence of life, because goodness is not defined by them. Though it is true that fame can be the blessing of God, for example, it is equally true that obscurity can be a precious gift. The two alternatives provide different challenges, but in either case the call to faithfulness remains constant.

It may surprise us to learn that our Western view of success is not appealing to everyone. Russian novelist Aleksandr Solzhenitsyn has this to say:

> Should someone ask me whether I would indicate the West such as it is today as a model to my country, frankly I would have to answer negatively. No, I could not recommend your society in its present state as an ideal for the transformation of ours. Through intense suffering our country has now achieved a spiritual development of such intensity that the Western system in its present state of spiritual exhaustion does not look attractive.[18]

This is not to suggest that suffering or deprivation is a virtue. But the Christian should realize that the way in which our society rewards success is not the only sign of the grace of God.

Faithfulness means trusting God enough to be content in any circumstance. When the apostle Paul issued a stern warning against seeking after riches, he pointed out that "godliness with contentment is great gain. For we brought nothing into the world, and we can take nothing out of it. But if we have food and clothing, we will be content with that" (1 Tim 6:6-8).

Such contentment is not a highly esteemed virtue today, even in Christian circles. Yet it is a mark of godliness which is not optional for the believer. Instead we tend to exhibit agitation and the conviction that our lot in life is simply not just. And notice the extreme to which Paul takes his teaching: "I have learned to be content whatever the circumstances. I know what it is to be in need, and I know what it is to have plenty. I have learned the secret of being content in any and every situation, whether well fed or hungry, whether living in plenty or in want" (Phil 4:11-12).

It's relatively easy to be content when we have plenty. That is hardly a notable achievement, though many of us fail even there. We need to examine ourselves. Are we content, even when in need? If not, why are we unwilling to trust the providence of God?

It is also important to recognize that some aspects of cultural success are at least partly dependent on the nature of our calling. It is possible, for example, for some in the business world to be given stewardship over a large amount of capital. Others, called into different spheres, may receive far less.

A friend of mine is owner and captain of a fishing boat off Nantucket Island. He provides employment for a half-dozen families and adds to the livelihood of dozens more. More money flows through his business in an average month than some of my artist friends will see all next year. Is this difference between the artist and the fisherman to be interpreted as an issue of success or failure for the Christian? Not at all—both might be equally faithful before God. Faithfulness is something money cannot measure.

In this abnormal world, some who are faithful before God in pursuing their calling may never see anything modern society (or the church) would identify as success. But we must not expect life to be fair until we get to heaven, and living as though we understand this frees us up to model Christian community. Being obedient even at personal cost is essential if the watching world is to see the love that proves we are disciples of Jesus Christ.

From the perspective of God's plan in history, what is vital is not whether our society rewards us. Rather, are we living to the glory and pleasure of God. We are not promised that lives of faithful obedience will be seen as successful in a fallen world. The rain falls on both the just and the unjust—and so do the droughts. We live for the praise of God, not the praise of other people.

Finally, Faithfulness

We will be held accountable for our response to God's blessings. Our Lord's standards are very high and consist of nothing less than his own holiness. Life is lived under the steady watchfulness of the God who is there, and that ought to move us to fear. Someday, we will have to answer for our choices, our priorities and our values. They had better be informed by more rigorous stuff than the passing measures of modern success.

Our faithfulness must be demonstrated in a marketplace charged with the desire for success and the fear of failure. What does it mean to pursue faithfulness before God in our vocation? Finding a practical answer is the subject of the next chapter.

Questions for Individuals and Groups

1. What changes in your thinking and life might be required since wealth, fame, power, self-fulfillment and appearance can be blessings from God? Why?

2. Have any of the measures of success been a testing of God in your life? If so, describe your experience.

3. How would you describe the difference between a testing of God and a temptation of the enemy?

4. What examples from the past or the present can you think of that further illustrate how these things have been used as God's judgment?

5. Wealth, fame, power, self-fulfillment and appearance can be both a) partly determined by the nature of our calling and b) unjustly distributed in a fallen world. What then is the Christian's responsibility? How can you incorporate this responsibility into your life?

6. Imagine trying to defend the biblical view of success to some non-Christian colleagues. How would you explain the four possible explanations to them?

How might they respond? How would you reply to their objections and questions?

If by doing some work which the undiscerning consider "not spiritual work" I can best help others, and I inwardly rebel, thinking it is the spiritual for which I crave, when in truth it is the interesting and exciting, then I know nothing of Calvary love.
Amy Carmichael

Why should I let the toad work
Squat on my life?
Can't I use my wit as a pitchfork
And drive the brute off?
Philip Larkin

Work is the curse of the drinking classes.
Oscar Wilde

CHAPTER 7

SEEING OUR WORK THE WAY GOD DOES

*W*hat do a professional mountaineer, Ferrari's top test-driver, the captain of the *QE2* and an underwater archaeologist have in common? According to *M: The Civilized Man* magazine, they all hold jobs most men fantasize about. Along with Ringo Starr and Chuck Yeager, these lucky souls are in "dream jobs." And what does a dream job consist of? "The dream job involves some combination of romance, power, money, satisfaction, or fun, in irresistible amounts."[1]

Perspectives on Work

Erroneous views of work flourish in modern Western society. Some, for example, see work as having no real meaning at all. Ingmar Bergman, highly acclaimed film director, exemplifies this view as he reflects on the meaning of life, work and art in his acceptance speech for the Erasmus Prize:

> Now, to be completely honest, I regard art (and not only the art of the cinema) as lacking importance.
>
> Literature, painting, music, the cinema, the theatre beget and give birth to themselves. New mutations and combinations emerge and are destroyed; seen from the outside, the movement possesses a nervous vitality—the magnificent zeal of artists to project, for themselves and an increasingly distracted public, pictures of a world that no longer asks what they think or believe. On a few preserves artists are punished, art is regarded as dangerous and worth stifling or steering. By and large, however, art is free, shameless, irresponsible, and, as I said, the movement is intense, almost feverish; it resembles, it seems to me, a snakeskin full of ants. The snake itself is long since dead, eaten out from within, deprived of its poison; but the skin moves, filled with busy life.[2]

This is not simply the rambling of a confirmed pessimist. If the horizons of life are bounded only by the cold emptiness of space and the finality of death, then there is no basis for significance. Our greatest work, our highest success amounts to nothing. The preacher of Ecclesiastes agrees: "I have seen all the things that are done under the sun; all of them are meaningless, a chasing after the wind" (Eccles 1:14).

At the other extreme, sometimes work is viewed in messianic terms. Not only is man's work meaningful, it will be mankind's salvation. Dr. M. Scott Peck, deeply influenced by New Age beliefs, exemplifies this viewpoint:[3]

> Discipline is the basic set of tools we require to solve life's problems. Without discipline we can solve nothing. With only some discipline we can solve only some problems. With total

discipline we can solve all problems.[4]

Peck has glimpsed something of the importance of work for human beings, but has taken that insight too far. His error is similar to that of the Israelites in Isaiah's day who thought all would be fine since their religious work never faltered. God told them it wasn't sufficient; all of their righteous efforts were actually detestable to him (Is 1:10-20).

Christians must reject both the undervaluing and the overvaluing of human work. Because God exists and because we're made in his image, our creative work is more than a snakeskin filled with ants. It is a God-given and God-blessed part of human life. Yet all the work in all the world over all of time will not restore us to Eden or usher in the Kingdom.

A Mistaken Christian View of Work

Mike and Janet's garden was something to behold. Long straight rows of vegetables: sweetcorn, green beans, cucumbers, squash, tomatoes, beetroots, carrots. The plants were lush and green, many of them bending over from the weight of the harvest. And not a weed in sight. Their back yard wasn't large, but through hard work our friends had transformed it into a place of productive beauty. Margie and I, on the other hand, had about given up on gardening. Weeds, aphids, mites, slugs, thistles, wilt and root rot—slowly we'd been beaten back. In this case, the Fall was getting the better of us.

I complimented Mike on their garden, but though he acknowledged my praise, his reply was mixed. He was proud of it, but he was uncomfortable too. "We don't spend too much time on it, you know," he said. "Just a couple of hours a week. I know there's lots more important things to be doing."

I replied that I could think of plenty of good reasons to

garden, but Mike wasn't satisfied. "After all," he continued, "we're Christians. Gardening has to be pretty far down the priority list. Why, if Christ came back today, most of the effort in this garden would've been wasted." Mike went on to explain that they planted a garden primarily to have a chance to witness. They shared with their neighbors when they took bags of fresh vegetables to them.

The issue Mike and Janet were wrestling with is an important one. They wanted to be faithful to Jesus Christ. They desired the work of their hands—even their gardening—to be pleasing to him. So they justified their gardening with witnessing. I remember thinking it was like mixing evangelism in with the manure to transform their garden into spiritual terrain. Although this sort of thinking is common among Christians, it represents a badly mistaken understanding of work, faithfulness and spirituality.

Recovering a Biblical Perspective

The Reformers, in contrast, taught that every legitimate vocation was pleasing to God. The baker and the minister, the printer and the scholar, the gardener and the carpenter—all were equally called by God, and each was to approach their work as service rendered to him. Every Christian had a calling or vocation before the Lord.[5]

Unfortunately, we've largely lost this heritage of clear biblical teaching. Christians today tend to speak in terms of careers or jobs, terms we've adopted from the world. When we do refer to a calling from God, we're usually referring to some sort of full-time ministry. What's more, few believers see their jobs as spiritual service. Like Mike and his garden, our careers are seen as secular but able to provide opportunities to do spiritual things, like evangelism rather than seeing gardening itself as spiritual.

What we've done without realizing it is embrace a secularized perspective on work. The fact that these opinions are cast in Christian terms only masks the problem. Dorothy L. Sayers, playwright and mystery novelist, was closer to the truth when she said, "The only Christian work is a good work well done." The Puritan William Perkins summarized the biblical teaching correctly when he said, "The main end of our lives . . . is to serve God in the serving of men in the works of our callings."[6]

If we're to think Christianly about success, about faithfulness in work, we'll need to recover a biblical perspective on the subject. I see seven main issues we need to cover on this topic. The first point to be made is a simple one, but for many Christians it represents a radical change. *Faithfulness in work means consciously approaching work as part of God's good creation for us.*

We won't understand work correctly unless we begin at Creation. Six times we are told in Genesis 1 that God examined what he had made and declared it good.[7] This applied to all he had called into being—not just to physical things like the stars, the plants and the animals. It also applied to work. Work was part of the created order for God's creatures, and it was good.

Work is not the result of the Fall, not something we're stuck with because Adam sinned. Created in the image of the Creator, we were made for it. We mustn't imagine that the ideal life would be one devoid of work. Life in the Garden was ideal, and Adam and Eve tilled the soil long before thistles became a problem. They were given a task to perform before the Fall took place (Gen 1:28). The Creator placed them in the Garden he had made particularly for them, and told them they were "to work it and take care of it" (Gen 2:15). They were to exercise creativity and to make changes that would reflect something of their ideas, their experiments and their personalities.

God's command also stressed that Adam and Eve were stewards in their work. The world in which they were to live remained the Lord's, and so it was important that they manage it with wisdom, affection and care. Their work was true service to him. Rooted in Creation, not the Fall, work provides both a fulfillment of our humanness and an opportunity to serve God.

No Sacred and Secular Divisions in Work

The second point to be made about work and faithfulness follows naturally from the first. *Every legitimate vocation is equally acceptable before God: There are no secular and sacred divisions in life for the Christian.* Contrary to popular opinion, the Bible never separates work into such categories. The Creator intended for us to live as physical creatures in a physical universe. "God's desire in delivering man out of lostness into fellowship with himself is to set us free to be human. Being human means being the people he originally intended us to be before the Fall—serving and enjoying him, serving and enjoying each other, ruling and enjoying his good world."[8]

Someday, the entire creation will be redeemed from the effects and curse of the Fall (Rom 8:18-25). Work is included in this, as service to God will not cease at the return of Christ, but will continue into eternity (Rev 22:3, 5; 1 Cor 6:2-3).

After Creation, "God took the man and put him in the Garden of Eden to work it and take care of it" (Gen 2:15). Adam and Eve worked, or cultivated, the garden.[9] They also cultivated a relationship with each other. They composed poetry, and used language imaginatively to structure, label and order the world (Gen 2:20, 23). They also cultivated a relationship with God. Human work produced human culture in obedience to God. All of this was part of being human, and all of it was pleasing—equally pleasing—to God.

As time went by, people progressed in obeying the cultural task given by God. Skills were developed and refined. Individuals began to specialize, passing their abilities and knowledge on to the next generation. Some became nomads, living in tents and raising livestock (Gen 4:20). Others learned to wrest metal from the ground, refine the ore and implement it (Gen 4:22). Still others become talented musicians. They invented musical instruments and filled the early world with the sounds of their art (Gen 4:21).

Further, the Bible teaches us that just as the physical universe is sustained by the Word of God, so also is human work and culture (Heb 1:3; Col 1:17). The Scriptures specifically speak of God's continuing creative activity not only in relation to the stars (Is 40:26), weather (Job 38) and animals (Job 39), but also to such human skills as farming (Is 28:24-29), crafts (Ex 31:2-5), metalwork (Is 54:16) and even warfare (Ps 144:1).[10]

Work is not an unfortunate interruption we must try to avoid in order to pursue more important endeavors. Work and human culture are not incidental to our faith, but foundational to our relationship with God as his creatures. He made us to live and work on the earth. The cultural mandate he gave remains in effect. To faithfully tend livestock or type letters or program software or raise children is as honorable—and as spiritual—as witnessing or prayer.

Being human is the nature of spiritual experience. Rejecting what is physical and despising it as unspiritual is a pagan idea.[11] William Tyndale had it right when he said, "There is difference betwixt washing of dishes and preaching of the word of God; but as touching to please God, none at all."[12]

When the Israelites were at Mount Sinai, God invited seventy-four of them to walk up the mountain to appear before him. So they "went up and saw the God of Israel. Under his feet was something like a pavement made of sapphire, clear as the sky itself. But God did not raise his hand against these leaders of the Israelites; they saw God, and they ate and drank" (Ex 24:9-11).

Seventy-four people find themselves before the face of him who is a consuming fire. And what do they do? They eat and drink. This so graphically illustrates our physicalness, our earthiness, our creatureliness. Even in the presence of God, that which is physical is not despised, but appreciated and accepted. They could bow in adoration and God would be pleased. They could pray and God would be pleased. And they could sit and eat their meal and this too would please God. Eating is a part of life as God intended in Creation and is spiritual, for like adoration, it is in his plan for us as his creatures.

God is not displeased with the physical but with sin. Since Christ is Lord of all, there is no dichotomy between physical and spiritual, secular and sacred. We must purge our minds and speech of notions such as *full-time service* and *secular careers*. All Christians are to be fully devoted to their Savior. Whether our vocation is in missions or astronomy, our Lord is only satisfied with lives that reflect full-time service to him.

Serving God in Our Work

When I first met Dan, he was a staff member with InterVarsity Christian Fellowship. He spent his days on college campuses bringing the truth of God to students. His time was filled with Bible studies, prayer meetings, discipling young believers, training Christian leaders and sharing the gospel with non-Christians. Later, Dan left IVCF to work on a ranch in Wyoming. Now his time is filled with cattle, hay, barbed-wire fences, branding and marketing beef. Less spiritual than campus ministry? Not at all. Less pleasing to his heavenly Father? Nonsense. *Faithfulness in work means that our work, regardless of our vocation, is to be rendered as obedient spiritual service to God.*

The early Puritans have much to teach us about this third point. They correctly insisted that the Christian must see "his shop as well as his chapel as holy ground," and that "every step and stroke in [his] trade is sanctified."[13]

I know another Dan, who is self-employed as an excavator in northern Minnesota. He has developed real expertise in digging cellars and septic tanks, grading roads and moving huge quantities of earth and rock. Good solid work, but hardly on most lists of spiritual ministries. He occasionally has a chance to witness and has attempted to be faithful in that. And he has consistently treated his customers and employees with honesty. These things are important, but his excavating doesn't need to be justified by evangelism and integrity. Employment that is not condemned by Scripture is acceptable as work. Those weeks when John is shut up for long hours alone in the cab of a truck are also service to God.

All that we do is to be understood and accomplished as unto the Lord. Paul even instructed slaves to fulfill their duties as unto him (Eph 6:5-8). When you witness to your neighbor or go to Korea as a missionary you serve God. And working as a baker, a teacher, a laborer, a soldier or in any other legitimate vocation is also serving God. In terms of pleasing and serving him, there is no difference.

What displeases God is not those vocations considered by misguided Christians as unspiritual. Disobedience is what displeases God. If we want to be faithful in our work, we must first be willing to be obedient to God's direction in our life. We must look to him to see what our life's work is to be. This is the fourth point. *Faithfulness in our work means being obedient to God's specific calling for our life.*

Calling

God directs us in two ways. First, there is his *general calling* to righteousness and obedience which is equally applicable to every believer. This is what we mean when we say that God desires every Christian to be like Christ. Most of what we need to know about life, morality and godliness we find in God's general call to us in his Word. It remains unchanged regardless of culture, personality or history.[14]

The second aspect of God's direction for us is particular to us alone. God's *specific calling* involves his direction for our vocation or life's work. Now there's no need to become mystical at this point. In relatively few instances in Scripture did God express his direction to his children through miraculous visitations.

His will is what matters, not his mode of communication. To think that a vision is finer than recognizing his sovereign hand in our circumstances is a failure of imagination. What does it suggest about us if we are insistent on receiving a momentary thrill? Our concern must be faithful obedience, not a seeking after spiritual highs.[15]

God is sovereignly at work in the midst of human history. We are part of God's redemptive plan and participants within the unfolding of his eternal purpose in Christ. Saved by grace, "we are God's workmanship, created in Christ Jesus to do good works, which God prepared in advance for us to do" (Eph 2:10).

Our specific calling places our gifts and work within the purposes of God in history.

God's specific calling gives us direction as his stewards on the earth. His calling fits us. The same one who calls us, made us (Jer 1:5). And it is in this calling that we can use our creativity, gifts and skills in obedient service.

The Importance of Calling

Gaining a sense of God's specific calling for us is strategic for a number of reasons. First, our calling gives us direction in a world overflowing with need. Without a sense of calling, we can be yanked about by every new need that comes along. Obedience is not the same as being manipulated by guilt over every new cause. Christ's lordship, not need, is to be our priority. Even our Lord didn't heal every leper in Israel. He knew what he was sent to do, and he could leave the rest to his Father.[16] This does not mean, of course, that we can be callous to the needs around us. Nevertheless, the direction of our lives should be geared not to the negative (needs) but to the positive (obedience to God's calling to us).

Second, God's specific calling also gives us a basis on which to say no to good things. One of the greatest pressures we face is becoming overextended. There are always more seminars to attend, non-Christians to witness to, causes to support, bodies to keep in shape, checkbooks to balance, lonely people to befriend, books to read, tapes to listen to. How do we establish clear priorities for our lives? How do we know what to say no to? It is by knowing what God has called us to say yes to. It can be disobedience to say yes to a good thing. The gospels record an episode where a man disobeyed by witnessing! Jesus told a leper he had healed to go to the priest as Old Testament law commanded. Instead the leper started telling people all over what had happened. The result was that the ministry of Christ was hindered because he couldn't enter the town openly (Mk 1:38-45).

Sometimes my wife and I are asked to do long-term counseling with people. We aren't gifted for such therapeutic relationships, and our calling and training are in other areas. So even though the request is for a good thing, we have the freedom to say no. It isn't that we don't care; we've simply come to see that, for us, obedience lies elsewhere.

Third, knowing our calling also saves us from being manipulated by the latest fads in the community. The pressure is great to conform to the social ideal of whatever group to which we belong. A sense of calling from God leads to a quiet assurance in the midst of pressure and criticism.

Gaining a Sense of Calling

God seems to communicate his specific calling to Christians in several ways. First, sometimes he speaks supernaturally, as he did to Paul when he was called to be an apostle to the Gentiles (Acts 9). This is a relatively rare but unmistakable way to hear God's calling.

For other people, God seems to communicate his special calling by placing within them a passion for some life's work. It seems to be part of their very being. I have known believers headed for science as well as missions who describe themselves this way. They almost seem to have been created for a single task.

For still other Christians, God seems to center a specific calling primarily around a spiritual gift. How they make their living is a relatively minor thing to them. Their heart's desire is to develop and use their gift for the glory of God and the building up of the Church.

But some Christians sense no particular passion for any vocation. Though gifted, they don't see their life centered around their spiritual gift. They may not even be sure God has directed them to where they are now, or to the vocation they find themselves in. They simply got there. They may not have even been concerned for God's direction in the past. Or they may feel thwarted by the fallenness of the world. Under circumstances such as this, it can be difficult to walk by faith. Yet even here we can—and we must.

When we are unsure about God's calling, it is wise not to make a change without clear direction from the Lord. Being faithful includes trusting his sovereignty in our lives. Walking by faith means believing his control over events is of such power that it is his hand which has brought us where we are. He created us, he formed us, he saved us and now he can use us. We aren't in our current situations by chance. It's good to ask him for a specific sense of calling. The real test, however, involves whether we are willing to be faithful to what he has made clear to us, regardless of how unclear other details remain.

What we should fear more than missing God's calling for our lives is rebelling against it. In the Scriptures there are illustrations of those who were called by God, but flatly refused to obey. Jonah is perhaps the best known example, and his disobedience was sinful and destructive. The Scriptures do not, however, contain a single example of God calling a willing servant who simply does not hear it. We mustn't agonize over missing God's direction in our life; we must exhibit our eagerness to faithfully serve him in obeying what he has revealed in his Word. The One who watches over sparrows hasn't forgotten us.

Asking the Lord for a sense of our specific calling (Jas 1:5) requires a willingness to be quiet before him. That discipline is little known in our age. Studying some of the passages of Scripture in which God calls his people can be instructive and encouraging.[17] Wise Christian friends can help confirm God's direction. Within Christian community we can be helped to identify evidences of God's grace in our life, determine our giftedness and help us sort out our heart's desire (Ps 37:4). We can also ask for prayer, perhaps the most valuable help of all.

Whether we can verbalize our specific calling or not, faithfulness in the present tense of life is the essence of discipleship. If you find yourself working in a bakery, gaining a sense of vocation won't necessarily mean you'll take up another line of work. It'll mean you faithfully bake bread as if your only customer were the Lord.

Pleasing God

The fifth point concerning work and faithfulness is that *the proper motivation for faithfulness in work is pleasing God.* "And whatever you do, whether in word or deed, do it all in the name of the Lord Jesus" (Col 3:17). This is why laziness is a sin.

Hard work doesn't necessarily result in success. It doesn't even guarantee we'll make a living. We are to work hard because we are servants of the King. When we sit down to dinner as a family, we stop to give thanks. We express our gratitude to God for providing for us and acknowledge that he is the only source of all good things. Our needs are met by the grace of God. William Perkins put it this way: "What, must we not labor in our callings to maintain our families? I answer: this must be done: but this is not the scope and end of our lives. The true end of our lives is to do service to God in serving of man."[18]

Both the work and the income are his good gifts.

Even making money is a form of obedience. The Puritans understood that "if God show you a way in which you may lawfully get more than in another way (without wrong to your soul, or to any other), if you refuse this, and choose the less gainful way, you cross one of the ends of your calling, and you refuse to be God's steward."[19]

Pleasing God means we will want our work to be marked with excellence. How can we possibly settle for less when our labor is done as obedience to Christ (Eph 6:7-8)? Just as we pray that our evangelism might bear fruit, so it is good to pray that the work of our hands would prosper and succeed to the Creator's glory.

Excellence includes working hard and conscientiously, giving the best that we can. It means applying creativity and humanness in the fulfillment of our responsibilities. It means being the sort of employee who knows what it is to actually work for the King.

We must grant freedom to one another as we wrestle with what it means for us to pursue excellence in our calling. Though the basic issues are the same for all of us, the specifics of faithfulness must be hammered out individually. Even those in the same profession can come to different conclusions before the Lord.

A physician we know, for example, believes he is called to pour the majority of his time and energy into his local church. The medical specialty he chose requires a minimum of hours. Though he works hard and with dedication as a casualty ward doctor, he is able to make a living by working only a few weekends each month. This doctor will probably never rise in the annals of the American Medical Association. But is this failure?

And the Christian physician who logs long days and nights at the hospital, and proportionately less time in church activities—is this different balance necessarily displeasing to God? The Scriptures give us no simple formula. Both physicians may be living lives of excellence before God.

Our work is to be done with all our strength. It is to be done as an expression of worship. Whatever our specific calling—whether it be in the arts, economics, theology, education, homemaking, business, crafts, science or farming—no matter what it is, we are to seek to please him in it. That is the only proper motivation for faithfulness in our work.

Vocation and Lordship

Pleasing God in our work means we must reflect holy standards of honesty, purity and personal righteousness. It also means our work must be submitted to his lordship. Thus, our sixth point: *Faithfulness in our work means our vocation itself must be under the rule of Christ.*

The truth of Scripture not only speaks to the morality of the scientist, it speaks to the nature of science. The Word of God not only addresses the honesty and kindness of the teacher; Creation, Fall and Redemption address theories of learning, knowledge and instruction. The lordship of Christ not only applies to the godliness of the musician, it provides a foundation for understanding art and aesthetics.

No matter what our work involves, we must learn to approach it from the perspective of the Word of God. The Christian physician, for instance, must realize that bringing Christ's lordship to medicine involves far more than placing religious magazines and books in the waiting room. He must develop a distinctly Christian basis for his ethics, business practices, relationships and models of health, illness and treatment. Each believer must likewise tackle his vocation as an expression of loving God with all his strength and soul and mind.

Modern society is teeming with unbiblical world views and mistaken assumptions about reality and life. Each vocation is dependent on and energized by sets of such assumptions. Most of the time they remain largely hidden. Seldom are they discussed and examined. Yet this is exactly what we must do if our work is to be under the rule of Christ. As James W. Sire has noted: "For any of us to be fully conscious intellectually we should not only be able to detect the world views of others but be aware of our own—why it is ours and why in the light of so many options we think it is true."[20]

Every sphere of human labor has assumptions and beliefs associated with it. In every case, these assumptions and beliefs have practical effects. The farmer adopts an attitude to the land on which he works. The person in business assumes standards for competing in the marketplace. Parents presuppose what is acceptable behavior for their children. The attorney approaches cases with beliefs about truth, guilt and justice. If the farmer sees the land as something he owns and can therefore exploit, this belief will affect how he farms. On the other hand, if he's deeply convinced the land is the Lord's, given to his care for a time as steward, he will make different choices.

The Enemy has infiltrated the Creation of God, and now we can work to uncover his lies and replace them with truth. "The weapons we fight with are not the weapons of the world. On the contrary, they have divine power to demolish strongholds. We demolish arguments and every pretension that sets itself up against the knowledge of God, and we take captive every thought to make it obedient to Christ" (2 Cor 10:4-5).

This is the Christian's call to arms. If this doesn't bring purpose to work, what will?

From Work to Toil: The Fall

Our service to God, regardless of our vocation, takes place in a fallen world. At the Fall, sin bent everything out of shape. Milton captured the moment well in *Paradise Lost*:

> . . . her rash hand in evil hour
> Forth reaching to the Fruit, she pluck'd, she eat:
> Earth felt the wound, and Nature from her seat
> Sighing through all her Works gave signs of woe,
> That all was lost.[21]

Everything was altered. Guilt and fault-finding intruded into human relationships and with God (Gen 3:12-13). Childbearing became dangerous and conception an ever-present possibility (Gen 3:16). And work was changed to toil:

> Cursed is the ground because of you;
> through painful toil you will eat of it
> all the days of your life.
> It will produce thorns and thistles for you,
> and you will eat the plants of the field.
> By the sweat of your brow
> you will eat your food
> until you return to the ground,
> since from it you were taken;
> for dust you are and to dust you will return.
> (Gen 3:17-19)

The Fall didn't remove the significance of our work, but it did twist work into something different from what God intended.

The Christian world view corresponds to what human beings have always understood about the nature of work. Work is a good thing and can be deeply satisfying, but it is also hard and unrelenting. The Bible gives us reason to value work without idolizing it and at the same time understand why work is tormented with hardship. Without a knowledge of Creation and the Fall, it is impossible to reconcile these seemingly contradictory aspects of work.[22]

Working in a fallen world means constantly leaning against the effects of the Fall. Just as we pull weeds in a garden, so we must labor to increasingly bring *shalom* to every aspect of creation that is under the curse of sin, including the workplace.

Jesus, who wept at the tomb of Lazarus, should be our model here (Jn 11).[23] He identified with those torn apart by the effects of the Fall. His was the deep emotion of those who can both grieve and rage at the result of sin. Jesus knew the time for the consummation of his kingdom had not arrived and after this resurrection, Lazarus would have to face death again. And so despite his grief, Jesus prayed, worked, resisted the effects of the Fall and brought life into the place of death.

Pushing back the Fall's effects can take many forms. Striving for justice in business, expanding employment, sharing the good news, helping to provide useful services or products, managing resources and people to bring efficiency out of chaos—these can all be redemptive tasks. Medicine and technology can be used to free humankind from some of the painful aspects of the curse. Entrepreneurs can create new business, freeing families from the pain of unemployment. Artists can open our eyes to aspects of truth we would otherwise miss. And missionaries and evangelists can tell the good news to people who have not yet heard it. Every legitimate vocation and trade pursued as service to God is part of the spiritual task of pushing back the Fall.

The Need for Balance

Finally, *faithfulness in work must be partially defined by the rest of what God has called us to do.* Though obedience in work is essential, the Creator doesn't see us as mere machines. Machines are made solely for accomplishing work. Men and women, though made for work, are also made for much more. Destroying one's family in order to climb the corporate ladder is hardly Christian faithfulness.

It would be relatively simple if each of us had only one thing to concentrate on. That isn't the way life is, though, and so we have to face the task of setting priorities and allocating time, energy and resources to a variety of responsibilities ordained for us by the Master.

God doesn't make mistakes. His callings are not destructive. Margie and I are convinced that if God has called me to travel in my work, then he has called our family to this as well. This means my travel need not be a great burden tearing away at the fabric of our relationships. This doesn't mean there isn't sacrifice involved or difficult times. There is. And I have had to learn to schedule things wisely so that my speaking is planned with the family in mind as well as my work. But since my calling embraces the entire family, dealing with my being away is also part of their calling before God. The same One who called me made us a family.

I am a writer and lecturer by vocation. If I am to please God in my work, I must strive for standards appropriate to godliness in my trade. But I am also called to be a husband, a father, a citizen, an elder in my church. Success in my work means I must be faithful to God in all that he has called me to do. And that faithfulness extends to all of my life as it is covered by his lordship.

This requires making difficult decisions. We need to resist the paralysis that can strike when we are faced with so many options. Life is too short and obedience too important to stay in a slump. There is too much at stake in the spiritual war to be found running endlessly from one part of the battle to another, wondering where to plunge in. Faithfulness means choosing boldly by faith.

We may need to regularly reevaluate our priorities and choices. Situations change and the decisions we made in the past may appear unwise or even impossible now. Commitments creep in to drown our schedule in waves of busyness. Needs show up that must be addressed. Map out on paper those things you believe God is calling you to do. Pray about striking the balance that faithfulness demands. Seek out points of weakness and make plans to grow.

One danger we need to be aware of is escapism, the temptation to use one part of our calling to escape other God-given responsibilities. I tend to find my vocation more satisfying than parenting, for example. Word processors and books don't backtalk, even on bad days. Few of us find every task equally enjoyable, and if we're not careful, that can become an excuse to disobediently spend time only on the ones we like best. Knowing that has helped me gain a better balance between work and home, and it has also helped Margie feel freer in leading the way at home, which she is more gifted at than I.

Faithfulness before God means we must be obedient across all of our life. Seeking a proper balance in a fallen world is never easy, but it is part of the Christian's responsibility. Success for the follower of Christ includes being faithful in work, responsibilities and calling, that part of life that takes up so much time and effort.

But there are other areas of life that must be marked by faithfulness. In the next chapter we'll examine three common but problematic areas and address them specifically. We'll determine what it means to be faithful in rest, in personal holiness and in the midst of failure.

Questions for Individuals and Groups

1. Where do you find examples of an overvaluing or undervaluing of work in modern society?

   What effects do such beliefs have?

2. What has shaped your view of work and how has it done this?

3. To what extent does your view resonate with a biblical perspective on work?

   Where exactly is it different and where in need of change?

4. How do Christians exhibit a dichotomy between the sacred and the secular in their lives?

   What effect does this have on the church's mission in the world?

5. What is your specific calling?

   What leads you to believe this is your calling?

6. What is (are) your spiritual gift(s)? How do you know?

7. What area of expertise or mastery have you developed or would you like to develop?

   What plans do you need to make to strengthen this area of your life?

8. How do you define excellence in your work? Why?

   What does your spouse or close friend think of your ideas on faithfulness and excellence?

9. How can we help our children grow up to gain a sense of God's calling for their lives? How can we help our friends?

On April 9, 1626, Francis Bacon climbed Highgate Hill in London, having decided on a scientific experiment. Here he ate a goose stuffed with snow to see whether the ice had halted the natural decay of the flesh. He died of typhoid.
David Frost

There will never be enough energy available to mankind from the atom to run a peanut whistle.
Robert Andrews Millikan

I do not think that a man can ever leave his business. He ought to think of it by day and dream of it by night. . . . Thinking men know that work is the salvation of the race, morally, physically, socially. Work does more than get us a living; it gets us a life.
Henry Ford

CHAPTER 8

FAITHFULNESS IN SOME TROUBLE SPOTS

The trouble began with mobs running riot in the streets.[1] Christians were attacked, houses ransacked, and the Roman officials in charge in France responded by throwing some of the Christians into prison. Blandina was only a young woman in A.D. 177 when the soldiers came to arrest her. A group of them were assigned to torture her, but though they wore themselves out, they failed to force her to deny her Lord.

The prisoners were kept in a dungeon, an unsanitary deathtrap so crowded that some died by suffocation. The Christians who survived were taken to the amphitheater. Blandina was among those who had wild animals set upon them. The majority perished, but Blandina lived to endure another day.

Some time later the survivors were taken to Lyons to be part of the grisly entertainment at a circus there. At the end of the day, only two remained alive: Blandina and a teenager named Plonticus. All the others had been burned alive, tortured by soldiers or torn to death by the animals. Finally, the sole survivors were overcome. Plonticus died under torture, and Blandina was battered unconscious by a wild bull and died. The Romans, awed by her fantastic courage, ordered around-the-clock guard over her body for six days before cremating it.

Blandina has joined all those who have gone before us to the finish line. Her part of the race is over. We are the ones to run the race now. "Therefore, since we are surrounded by such a great cloud of witnesses, let us throw off everything that hinders and the sin that so easily entangles, and let us run with perseverance the race marked out for us" (Heb 12:1).

The race that we are called to is marked by a different type of faithfulness, a different perseverance than Blandina's. But this must not blind us to what remains the same. Like Blandina, we live each moment before the face of God. In faithfulness to him, we find his pleasure and true success.

Our goal must be to please God in all that we do. In the last chapter we explored what that means in our work and calling. Our discipleship extends to our being family members, workers, citizens and members of the church. Being faithful means we will need to be sure we are making progress in applying Christ's lordship to each area in which we have responsibility. God's call to us in the whole of life, in work and beyond, is the essence of our discipleship.

In this chapter we'll continue to explore the nature of faithfulness in a fallen world. We'll examine three common problem areas for Christians living at the end of the twentieth century: being faithful in resting as God has commanded, being faithful in personal holiness and being faithful in failure.

Being Faithful in Rest

We've seen that our work is significant to God. Contrary to popular opinion, so is our rest. I have trouble with setting aside my work, even for short periods. I remember the time I came to the supper table distracted by my work. Conversation began as we sat down to supper, and I helped pass around the food. But apparently my preoccupation had rendered me deaf, because I looked up to find my family glaring at me. Someone had asked me a question and I hadn't responded. I was chagrined as my youngest daughter said: "Oh, don't feel bad. Dad just *looks* like he's here."

My struggle with preoccupation is just one manifestation of my struggle with rest. I like my work, I fancy it to be important and the satisfaction I receive from it makes it difficult for me to set it aside. Yet, as Paul Marshall points out: "Our work has, per se, no prior claim to our time."[2]

Actually, my problem with rest is a common one. Take Jeanne Rogers, for instance. At thirty-three years of age, she is only one of four women in Illinois to have achieved the designation of Certified Commercial Investment Member. Reflecting on her use of time, she says:

During October of 1984 to March of 1985 [that's 6 months, by the way], I did $6 million in business transactions, had a baby in December and was back to work two days after leaving the hospital. . . . My son and husband make my work easier because it forces me to be more efficient. I use my car phone, take work home and limit my hours from 7 a.m. to 7 p.m. It's a matter of using your time efficiently. I closed a deal while I was in labor with Nicholas.[3]

Recovering a Biblical View of Rest

In Scripture we find that rest is not optional for Christians. Faithfulness means accepting all the responsibilities God has given us, but work is just one part of that. Rest, like work, is also rooted in Creation, not in the Fall (Gen 2:1-3). It needs to be part of our lives not because we're sinners, but because we are made in the likeness of the One who rested. We were made for rest. When we rest, we manifest something of God's image that can not be demonstrated in any other way.

The importance of rest is further emphasized in the Law given at Sinai (Ex 20:8-11). Here God expanded on the creational order, codifying it for the nation of Israel. "The commandment not to labour on the Sabbath carries as much weight as the commandments not to kill or steal. . . . Israel's life was ordained as a rhythm of work and rest. Each seventh day, each seventh year and each seventh of seven years was a Sabbath for people, for animals and for the land itself."[4]

The reason rest is so hard in a fallen world is its link to faith. In the Old Testament, God ordained that every seven years Israel was to refrain from planting crops. It was to be a Sabbath year, a year of rest. "If Israel rested in the seventh year, it needed to trust in God's promise that the land would produce a surplus to see them through (Lev 25:18-24). In the fiftieth year, the year of Jubilee, Israel's faith was tested even more. As they celebrated the Day of Atonement they needed to put aside the work of their hands for two years: they would live off the gifts of God (Lev 25:8-12)."[5]

Israel understood that unbelief, or lack of trust, would end in a lack of rest (Ps 95:8-11).

Faith and rest are tied in the New Testament as well. Salvation and rest are used as pictures of each other. Jesus invited all those "who are weary and burdened" to come to him. The implications of this passage are not very flattering. Jesus sees us as so many oxen, milling about with ill-fitting yokes, hopelessly overburdened. "Come," he gently says, "and I will give you rest" (Mt 11:28-30).

> When we rest we acknowledge that all our striving will, of itself, do nothing. It means letting the world pass us by for a time. Genuine rest requires acknowledgement that God, and our brothers and sisters, can survive without us. It requires a recognition of our own insufficiency and a handing over of responsibility. It is a real surrender to the ways of God. It is a moment of celebration when we acknowledge that blessing comes only from the hand of God. That is why rest requires faith.[6]

When we think that the world or the church will grind to a halt if we set aside our labor to rest, we think too highly of ourselves. Once when I was a young staff member with InterVarsity, my supervisor came for a visit. For three days he evaluated my work on campus. Then, as he was about to leave, he had one more comment. "I think it'd be good," he said as he put his arm around my shoulders, "if you stopped thinking of yourself as the Messiah." His comment prompted me to recognize my limitations. As I learned to give my InterVarsity group over to God more and to the members, I became a more effective chapter leader and a more peaceful servant in God's kingdom.

Working on Rest

Rest is a good gift, a facet of our humanness through which we can creatively manifest God to a watching world. And as we make regular rest a priority, God can manifest himself to us in new ways as he stretches our faith.

Biblical rest should not be confused with mere leisure. Rest is temporarily setting aside work in an act of trust in God's sovereign providence. Leisure, on the other hand, consists of entertainment. This doesn't mean that leisure is sinful or that rest can never include fun. But they aren't synonymous. Leisure can be an escape, but rest never is. Leisure can be passive, but rest involves an active, vibrant trust. Leisure is often a recuperation from or preparation for work—implying that work is the central concern. Rest does not derive its meaning from work. It is significant in its own right. Rest needs no justification.

Faithfulness in resting is not a matter of meriting the grace of God or of chalking up cosmic brownie points. It need not become legalistic.[7] Jesus warned about this when he observed that the Sabbath was made for man, not man for the Sabbath (Mk 2:27).

We pay a price when we are unfaithful in rest. Abraham Kuyper, a theologian and statesman, so overworked himself that his health failed. For fifteen months he was ill. His collapse was so great that at first he didn't have the strength to write so much as a postcard.[8] After his recovery, he wisely added rest to his schedule. He went on to found the Free University of Amsterdam and to become prime minister of Holland in 1901.

There are times when rest is particularly difficult. Junior hospital doctors often have minimal control of their time. Parents with young children may have continual demands placed on them. We need to remind ourselves who it is that we serve and that he understands our circumstances. God is a gentle Shepherd who created our finiteness (Is 40:11). Jesus knows what it means to be exhausted (Mk 4:38). The rest we experience here in this fallen world will always be incomplete. Our true and complete rest is still to come.

From the perspective of Scripture, to be disobedient concerning rest is to fail in something God has ordained for us. We should evaluate our lives and build cycles of work and rest into our schedule.[9] Beginning each day in prayer, praise and the reading of Scripture can bring a quiet which can help to temper the busyness of the day. Perhaps that's one reason why it's called a *quiet time*. To foster this is wise.

Made in the likeness of the God who rested, we are to image him. We cannot do that as he intends if rest is squeezed out of our lives. As we think Christianly about success, we will realize that faithfulness before God includes trusting him enough to regularly set aside our work and responsibly rest in him.

Being Faithful in Personal Holiness

Success for the Christian consists of a life of faithfulness to God and his Word. His calling to us is a call to walk in personal holiness.[10] "Just as he who called you is holy," Peter tells us, "so be holy in all you do; for it is written: 'Be holy, because I am holy' " (1 Pet 1:15-16).

Personal holiness must be part of a Christian's view of success. Though God's image in man was not erased in the Fall, it was badly distorted. Now through Christ there can be a substantial restoration as by God's grace we are changed into the very likeness of Christ. As we contemplate his glory, Paul tells us, we "are being transformed into his likeness with ever-increasing glory" (2 Cor 3:18).

Personal holiness includes learning to love God with our minds: "Do not conform any longer to the pattern of this world, but be transformed by the renewing of your mind. Then you will be able to test and approve what God's will is—his good, pleasing, and perfect will" (Rom 12:2). Moment by moment, a choice faces us. Either we are living transformed lives or lives that are molded by the world. Conformity to the pattern of the world can hardly be the mark of success for a child of God. That's true even if the world thinks it's wonderful.

Our minds must be steeped in Scripture. The goal is not to regurgitate verses on command. Rather we must seek to have our thinking, our vision, our mindset, our very consciousness brought into conformity with the revealed mind and will of God.[11]

In other words, we must, by God's grace, learn to think Christianly. Os Guinness defines it, "Thinking Christianly is thinking by Christians about anything at all in a profoundly Christian way. Where their minds are so informed and influenced by the truth of God in terms of their principles, perspectives, and presuppositions that they begin to see as God sees, though in an imperfect way."[12]

How I think about things sets my priorities, alters my values, influences my relationships and flows out in practical ways into all that I do and say. It is as important for parents to think Christianly about Saturday morning cartoons as it is for a physicist to think Christianly about science.

The apostle says that it is the renewed mind that will be a discerning one: "Then you will be able," Paul wrote, "to test and approve what God's will is" (Rom 12:2). Developing skill in discernment is essential for the believer living in a pluralistic society. Around us swirls a confusing mental marketplace of world views and beliefs. As Western society searches for ethics in an age of failed relativism and struggles for meaning amid uncertain success, Christians must be able to make clear distinctions. Discernment means being able to identify what is being communicated, critique it in the light of Scripture and respond in a godly manner.

One of the concerns Margie and I have had as parents is to raise our children to be discerning people. Lectures, books, news magazines, TV, films, music and advertising barrage us all. Unspoken assumptions and world views lie behind each of them. It is simply impossible to try to shelter our children as if they will never need to face any of it. And it is also impossible to cover every possible combination of faulty belief that might come up in the future. What is possible is to develop the skills needed to uncover world views and reflect on them biblically.

Faithfulness mandates intellectual holiness. As Donald Drew was fond of saying, "You probably aren't what you think you are, but what you think, you are." Loving God with our minds includes being discerning enough that we are not tossed about by every wind of doctrine.

A Relationship with a Holy God

Personal holiness also means a growing intimacy with our heavenly Father. Christ died so that we might have a personal relationship with God. There's a big difference between knowing him and only knowing about him.

The difference is well illustrated when Abraham discussed with the Lord the impending destruction of Sodom and Gomorrah (Gen 18). Six times Abraham speaks up, pressing for details concerning the Lord's plan. Amazingly, it was the Lord who had initiated the subject: "Then the LORD said, 'Shall I hide from Abraham what I am about to do?' " (v 17). Imagine: "The Lord of far-flung galaxies, the Creator of life and of all that exists, the All-Powerful, the All-Knowing, the Inscrutable, the Judge of angels, demons and people is taking the trouble to explain his actions to an individual and is talking to him without condescension, but in terms that he can understand."[13]

God has this conversation with Abraham because, he tells us, Abraham is his friend. That should remind us of what Christ said to his disciples. "You are my friends," the Lord said, "if you do what I command." The implications of this are incredible:

> Two facts necessarily follow. If you are his friend, he will share his thoughts and plans with you. If you are his partner, he will be concerned about your views on his plans and projects. Whatever else prayer may be, it is intended to be a sharing and a taking counsel with God on matters of importance to him. God has called you to attend a celestial board meeting to deliberate with him on matters of destiny.
>
> You can see at once how this raises the whole level of prayer. It is not intended primarily to be centered in my petty needs and woes. To be sure, God is interested in them. They have a place on his agenda. But the agenda itself has been drawn up in heaven and deals with matters of greatest consequence.[14]

Do we grasp anything of the wonder of this? Throughout history there have been those who have developed a growing intimacy with God. They have taken seriously the personalness of our heavenly Father. No understanding of success can have significance if it is devoid of this. What is worth having if we do not know the living God, if we do not walk with him day by day?

Faithfulness in Failure

The settlers living in southern Minnesota were still a bit jumpy. Only four years previously, in 1862, the Sioux uprising led by Little Crow had resulted in massacres on both sides.[15]

On the afternoon of April 19, 1866, Sam Brown received word

that a new outbreak of violence was imminent. Indian tracks had been discovered heading toward the Minnesota territorial line. Brown quickly dispatched a warning letter to Army scout headquarters in St. Paul and stopped by Fort Wadsworth to tell the commander to prepare for war. Then Brown took off on his strongest horse to warn the scouting station at Elm River, and to spread the alarm to all the settlers en route.

Leaving at sundown, Brown raced through the night, wondering all the way if he would be suddenly ambushed and killed. Not stopping to rest, he covered the sixty miles in about five hours. Thanks to him, all the settlers in the area knew of the danger and were busy preparing to fight. Leaping from his exhausted animal, Brown awakened the chief of the scouts at the Elm River Station and told him the news.

Nonsense, replied the scout chief. There's no danger. In fact, the Indian tracks must have been from the special Indian peace delegation which was traveling north through that area.

"Imagine my mortification!" Sam Brown later said.[16] Since his false alarm now put innocent people in danger, Brown took a fresh horse and began the return journey. The sky clouded over, and he no longer had the stars to guide him. Occasional lightning flashes split the blackness. Then the storm broke with first a lashing rain, then with sleet and finally a driving snow. Twice as he raced along the James River his pony slipped, throwing him off into the icy water. Thankfully Brown had thought to fasten his lariat to the bridle, tying the other end to his belt.

About daybreak, Sam recognized his surroundings. He was fifteen miles off course and nearly frozen. Brown finally reached Fort Wadsworth around eight o'clock in the morning, where he collapsed, unconscious. Sam's "great adventure," as he called it, had consisted of galloping one hundred and fifty feverish miles on horseback for nothing.[17]

Thankfully, not every failure is as spectacular as that. But one thing is certain: we've all failed. No one escapes that. In the most fundamental sense we have failed: "There is no difference," the apostle Paul wrote, "for all have sinned and fall short of the glory of God" (Rom 3:23). We are all included here. Our failure before the holiness of God is as absolute, and as deadly, as failure can be.

Two Who Failed

Read again the story of Judas Iscariot.[18] What did he think and feel when Jesus stooped to wash his feet? Did he understand what the Lord meant when he said, "you are clean, though not every one of you" (Jn 13:10)? Did he have second thoughts when Jesus handed him the piece of bread?

"As soon as Judas had taken the bread, he went out," we are told. "And it was night" (Jn 13:30). It must have been lonely. Jerusalem was crowded with visitors for the Passover, but the streets would be deserted and still as families observed the Jewish feast.[19] But Judas, like the lepers, was now outside the warmth of community and away from the Passover Lamb.

His choice was made; a bribe had been taken. Judas kissed the One who had washed his feet. Jesus was led off and the circle of disciples scattered in disarray.

> When Judas, who had betrayed him, saw that Jesus was condemned, he was seized with remorse and returned the thirty silver coins to the chief priests and the elders.
>
> "I have sinned," he said, "for I have betrayed innocent blood."
>
> "What is that to us?" they replied. "That's your responsibility."

So Judas threw the money into the temple and left. Then
he went away and hanged himself. (Mt 27:3-5)

Such is the failure of sin. Its end is death.

Now think also of Peter, who struggled with failure on the same evening as Judas.[20] Both had failed to be faithful. As with Judas, Jesus revealed that he knew what Peter was about to do.

"I tell you the truth," Jesus told him, "this very night, before the rooster crows, you will disown me three times" (Mt 26:34). Peter was sure the Lord was mistaken. Why, just moments before when Jesus stooped to wash Peter's feet he had objected! It wasn't proper for the Master to serve the disciple, he thought. When Jesus replied "Unless I wash you, you have no part with me" (Jn 13:8), Peter requested a complete bath. That turned out to be an improper suggestion, but it did reveal that his heart was in the right place.

We see more of Peter's commitment to Christ in the impulsive use of his sword in Gethsemane. He struck a servant of the high priest, "cutting off his ear" (Mk 14:47). No doubt Peter was aiming for the center of the man's skull. And Peter's devotion is evident again in his decision to follow the crowd that took Jesus away. I suspect Peter was determined to prove Jesus wrong in his prediction of unfaithfulness. But Peter failed (Mt 26:69-75).

Perhaps the first accusation of association with Jesus took him by surprise. Who would have expected a servant girl to say such a thing? "I don't know what you're talking about," he retorted (Mt 26:70). Then, as Peter moved toward the gate, another girl spoke up. "This fellow was with Jesus of Nazareth" (Mt 26:71). Peter denied it again, this time with some well-chosen oaths. The third accusation was a clever trap. "Surely you are one of them," someone said, "for your accent gives you away" (Mt

26:73). This time, as Peter spat out his vulgar denial, the sharp, unmistakable voice of a rooster split the night.

All four Gospel writers include Peter's story, but Luke adds a jolting detail. At the very moment the rooster began to crow, the "Lord turned and looked straight at Peter." (Lk 22:61). He had failed his Master utterly, and the Lord had been watching.

Every Sin Is Failure

Not every failure is a sin, but every sin is failure. Sin is failing to measure up to God's glory (Rom 3:23). The most common words translated "sin" (Hb: *chattath, chet;* Gk: *hamartia*) both mean "missing the mark" and cover the ideas of "erring" or "failure."[21] It is God himself who is the final reference point for our failure-as-sin.

Every sin is failure because it represents a falling short of that for which we were created. Our natural state is not sin, but holiness. When someone excuses their sin by saying, "Well, I'm only human," we understand what they mean. But if we wish to see human beings as they were meant to be, we must look at Eve and Adam before they disobeyed. We were created for holiness. The Fall and its wake of sin came after Creation.

But the Fall has given us the reality and the feeling of guilt. Last summer, as I was making last-minute preparations to lead a discussion group, my son, looking agitated, said he had something to tell me. I was preoccupied with my work, and so was only half-listening when the words "sorry," "cigarette lighter," "firecracker" and "alley" entered my consciousness. I was furious. I ranted at him, issued a punishment and dismissed him from the room.

Within a few minutes my guilt caught up with me. For one thing, I should have been pleased by my son's honesty. He could have kept quiet, and chances are I would have never known. For another thing, it was almost the Fourth of July, and he had shown himself to be responsible up to that point. I was concerned for his safety, but my reaction still was out of line. Much of my anger was irritation at being interrupted. Didn't my son rate more than that? I felt defeated by how often I had had to deal with the sin of treating my family as an interruption. I had sinned against my son and needed to seek his forgiveness. But more foundationally, I had sinned against God (Ps 51:4).

The Solution to Guilt

Failure-as-sin is a moral issue, and God's provision for it is redemption through the finished work of Jesus Christ on the cross. Nothing else will do. Only this will remove true moral guilt before a righteous God. "The wages of sin," we are told, "is death" (Rom 6:23). Our sin has been judged in the person of Christ, not merely overlooked or ignored. In his sacrificial death on our behalf, true forgiveness is ours as the gift of God.[22]

After Peter's denial, Jesus was tortured, crucified and buried. Three days passed. Early Sunday morning some women went to his tomb and instead of a body, they found an angel: " 'Don't be alarmed,' he said. 'You are looking for Jesus the Nazarene, who was crucified. He has risen! He is not here. See the place where they laid him. But go, tell his disciples and Peter' " (Mk 16:6-7).

Notice the last few words of the angel's message. Not just "go tell his disciples," which would have included Peter, but "go tell his disciples *and Peter*." Go tell Jesus' followers about what has taken place—and make sure Peter hears. Jesus Christ had paid the penalty for Peter's sin.

Forgiveness is as deeply personal as the fateful moment when

Peter looked into the eyes of his Lord. Peter had failed, but Jesus hadn't. The substitutionary death of Christ provided the solution to Peter's failure, to his guilt and sin—and to ours.

Not All Failure Is Sin

All sin is failure, but not all that we call failure is sin. We're both fallen and finite. Both represent limits, limits that we come up against every day. God is never pleased with our fallenness and is never displeased with our finiteness. Even in heaven we will remain finite, because only God is infinite (Ps 90:2, Is 45:6, 2 Cor 5:1-6). When our failure is rooted in our fallenness, it is sin. But often we say we've failed when no rebellion against God is present: we have simply come up against our finiteness.

When our plans go awry or when carefully made goals turn out to be unrealistic, we say we've failed. One day I needed to make a bank deposit, drop mail at the post office and rent a videotape for the film discussion we were hosting that evening. An hour, ninety minutes at the outside, would surely be enough time. At the bank I chose the shortest long line and ended up behind a little old lady who had six transactions to perform. Every one had to be dug separately out of her handbag—a handbag stuffed with papers. She hadn't even endorsed the cheques ahead of time or filled out the deposit slips. Then the man at the post office took two personal phone calls while I stood there. The video shop didn't have the film I was looking for. Yes, they had reserved it for me. Yes, they were sorry. Yes, I had to go to four other shops before I found it.

Three simple errands that should have been finished in an hour had taken me all afternoon. I called the afternoon a "failure," but was this guilt necessary? Did I need to repent before God?

And what about when we lack knowledge or skill in some area? We might do our best, but still come up short and fail. Repairing the car often leads to this sort of disaster for me. Bolts turn out to be rusty and stripped, the tool needed for the job is one I don't own, and small parts tend to fall into dark crevices. I may respond sinfully in this situation, of course, but is my lack of skill a matter of sin?

At Creation, God told Adam and Eve they were to have dominion on the earth (Gen 1:28-30). God created human beings to be his agents of change in the world. Our sense of personal identity can suffer if we can point to no area in life within which we have some sense of mastery or expertise. Also we may feel we have failed if we do not measure up to the models we have adopted for ourselves (consciously or unconsciously). To fail to live up to our internal standards can be a jolting experience. And even if those models change or are foolish or unrighteous, they remain important to our personal sense of success or failure.

But does failing to meet our own standards necessarily constitute sin?

Unrealistic goals, lack of knowledge, no sense of personal mastery or expertise in life, falling short of internal standards—these are some of the things that we define as failure, yet they are not equivalent to sin. Failing to measure up to our expectations is never pleasant, but need not be mistaken for wickedness.

Dealing with Failure

Faithfulness in the midst of failure means distinguishing between sin and personal failure. Being mistaken about how long an essay is going to take is not a sin, even if we call the episode a failure. Punching your flatmate because you feel bad about it, is. Fallenness and finitude are different, and we need to treat them accordingly and keep our conscience from being cluttered up with false guilt.

Part of our struggle with failure boils down to refusing to accept our finiteness as a good gift of God. He created us to live in twenty-four-hour days and called that arrangement good. Rebelling against God's will in this is both evil and futile.

Growing in faithfulness in the face of failure includes learning to distinguish between guilt and shame. They both describe falling short of a standard. Guilt is related to a moral standard. It comes from failure-as-sin. Shame, on the other hand, is related to the "kind of notion in our minds of the person we would like to be."[23] Shame can be present when there is no sin to confess. Although shame and guilt might feel identical, they are not. Consider their opposites: "The opposite of guilt is innocence or moral purity. The opposite of shame, though, is not innocence; it is honor and glory."[24]

The biblical solutions for guilt and shame differ.[25] We've already seen that the answer to true moral guilt, to failure-as-sin, is redemption. Confessing our sin means agreeing with God's assessment and facing up to the reality of our failure (1 Jn 1:9). And when failure-as-sin involves other people, confession, making restitution and even church discipline are all part of God's provision to free us from the guilt that would remain as an albatross around our necks. Relief from guilt also means we must believe God's promise that our sin has been reversed in Christ.[26]

The solution God gives to shame is also rooted in Jesus Christ and his finished work. We not only have forgiveness in Christ, we have personal acceptance before God through him. Forgiveness gets to the heart of guilt. Acceptance gets to the heart of shame.

We are adopted as sons and daughters of God and are invited to call him Abba. He is not only Judge, but Father as well. We are granted unconditional acceptance in the present and the hope of glorification for the future. The day will come when he "will replace our shame with honor and glory."[27]

We can look forward to that day with great hopefulness. The King will return soon, and it is at his coming that the true nature of success will be finally revealed. In the meantime, what is the proper motivation for our lives? Being energized by the lure of cultural success is hardly adequate. How we should live as we wait is the subject of the next chapter.

Questions for Individuals and Groups

1. What attitudes toward rest did you grow up with?

2. What is your attitude and practice now?

3. What would you say is the difference between rest and leisure? Between rest and laziness?

4. In the film *Chariots of Fire,* part of Eric Liddell's witness in his running was his refusal to race on Sunday. Should the Christian set aside one day in seven as a special sabbath rest? Why or why not? (Are your reasons simply your opinion, or can you defend them from Scripture?)

5. What are the stumbling blocks in your life in maintaining a proper balance between work and rest? How do they reveal a lack of faith?

6. To what extent are you characterized by a growing intimacy with your heavenly Father?

What is keeping you from developing a closer relationship?

7. Some have said modern Christians are less sensitive to sin than their forebears. Do you agree? Explain.

To what extent do we have trouble dealing with guilt, sin and forgiveness? How can we help one another grow in this area?

8. Discuss the difference between shame and guilt. How and when do they overlap?

9. What models for personal success do you have?

Where did you get them?

10. Where do you struggle with the standard these models set for you? To what extent are they godly models?

11. What models are pushed on you by family, by your profession or by your friends, and what is a Christian response?

12. What specific plans should you make to become more faithful in rest? in personal holiness? in failure?

What do people mean when they say "I am not afraid of God
because I know He is good"? Have they never been to a dentist?
C. S. Lewis

The holiness of God is injured by our unprepared addresses to
him, when, like swine, we come into the presence of God with all
our mire reeking and steaming upon us.
Stephen Charnock

It is in our hearts that
the evil lies,
and is from our hearts that
it must be plucked out.
Bertrand Russell

CHAPTER 9

WHAT THE WORLD DIDN'T TELL YOU ABOUT MOTIVATION

Suzi is a musician, but it can be hard to make a living playing the cello. A graduate of the Eastman School of Music, she spent several years as a member of the symphony orchestra of Caracas, Venezuela. Then oil revenues dipped, Venezuelans had less money, and Suzi needed to find other work.

Finances hadn't been the only pressure. A Christian, Suzi had long been criticized by fellow believers for pursuing music. Couldn't she find something more "practical and useful" to do with her life? Then there was the cost of her instrument. Good cellos cost thousands of dollars, and hundreds more to maintain. How could someone who had seen the poverty in South America justify those expenditures?

Suzi finally decided to set aside the cello and head for medical school. Being a physician would provide a steady income and make her part of a helping profession. Surely she could do this with a clear conscience! As Suzi applied herself to her studies, she found she enjoyed them. The demands of learning were vigorous, but clearly within her reach. But there was a problem—Suzi's heart still belonged to her now-silent cello.

We sat down more than once to talk and pray about what she should do. Either way, the choice was a difficult one. Although I couldn't tell Suzi what God's will was for her, I could tell her that no matter how much she concentrated on medicine, nothing lit her eyes up like her cello. I had no doubt Suzi could make a good physician or that God could use her in medicine. But I joined her in doubting whether God was calling her to leave music.

Together we reviewed her dilemma. All of Suzi's life had centered on her art. The challenge of long, strenuous hours of practice was welcomed. In every church she had belonged to, Suzi helped make music a part of the congregation's life, worship and ministry.

Her cello was a finely crafted instrument. We marveled at its beauty and reflected on its value. In a world where death and decay destroy all that is beautiful and good, wasn't the preservation of a fine cello over so many years a very precious thing?

Yet if she gave herself to the cello there was no guarantee she would be able to make a living. If she did manage to land a good position she could look forward to the intense competition of the music profession.

Suzi isn't in medicine today. She's playing the cello. The struggles of income and criticism still remain, and the demands of her vocation are wearisome at times. Such is Suzi's cost of discipleship. Whatever our call, we can expect to face difficulties if we follow Jesus Christ. To struggle is not a sign of failure.

Our Need: Motivation to Keep On

It is one thing to determine to please God, but it's quite another to maintain that zeal in the middle of the race. The finish line seems miles away, and the hurdles we have to jump multiply until the running feels impossible. We mean to keep on, of course, but faithfulness is not easy. If we're to remain faithful in this fallen world, we desperately need a holy spirited motivation to keep us from giving up. What is to be our motivation to please God? What is to keep us keeping on?

Often, the primary motivation in our lives is guilt. Guilt pops up everywhere: We may choose a simple lifestyle because we feel guilty about hunger overseas. We may choose to witness because we feel guilty about knowing someone for six months at work without Christianity even coming up. We may have a regular quiet time less out of a desire to know God than to silence our nagging conscience.

Last summer my wife was asked to help teach at a holiday Bible club. We decided, after praying about it, that she should say no. Her gifts could be better used elsewhere, and we had already made plans for those dates. Still, it was very hard to call our pastor's wife and say no. Somehow it sounded identical to saying: "No, I'm not willing to help out. I won't change my plans. I'm unwilling to share in the life and work and evangelism of the church. And what's more, I don't really care if the kids hear the gospel or not."

It can be difficult to silence the voices of guilt. Too often we make commitments not because we're convinced obedience demands it, but because we feel guilty saying no. Guilt is an unhealthy and improper motivation for the Christian life. The

Holy Spirit can convict us of sin, of course, and the experience of guilt can contribute to our willingness to repent. Nevertheless, Christ died to remove our guilt. Living in obedience to his lordship is quite different from being endlessly yanked around by guilt. The child of God should be able to learn of needs without collapsing into spasms of guilt feelings. Hearing of fields that are white with harvest should move us to prayer, not tie us in knots (Mt 9:38). Guilt is a common, but wholly inadequate, motivation for faithfulness. A Christian desire for success in the eyes of God requires more than that.

Another common motivation that appears in Christian circles is the promise of happiness. If we are faithful, we're told, joy and fulfillment are sure to follow. My youngest daughter recently brought home a handout from school which illustrated this idea. "Do something nice for someone every day," it said. "It will make you happy, too." That may sound good, but it simply isn't true. I agree there is joy in obedience, and I also agree our deepest fulfillment comes in faithfulness to God. But I also know that sometimes the obedience is widely separated from the reward. In some cases faithfulness is met by hardship, and the joy must wait, perhaps until heaven. We need to be obedient because it's right, whether we feel happy about it or not.

What is the proper motivation for a successful life before God? Scripture gives us the answer.[1] There is something that deeply stirs our hearts and minds as we look forward to the return of the King. It is powerful enough to bring us through the hardest times and natural enough to be within the experience of every Christian who is willing to bow before God. It is, in fact, the natural response of any person who comes face to face with the risen Savior and Lord. What is this experience which will motivate us to faithfulness?

It is *the fear of the Lord and the love of Christ.*

But aren't fear and love opposed to each other? Not necessarily and certainly not in Christ. When the apostle John saw the glorified Christ, he "fell at his feet as though dead" even as the Lord touched him and gently told him not to be afraid (Rev 1:17). To understand Calvary is to understand both the holy judgment of God and the depths of his grace. It is to be filled with love for the One who gladly suffered in our place, even as we are overwhelmed at his white-hot wrath against sin.

John Calvin observed that because the Christian mind

> ... sees him to be a righteous judge, armed with severity to punish wickedness, it ever holds his judgment seat before its gaze, and through fear of him restrains itself from provoking his anger. And yet it is not so terrified by the awareness of his judgment as to wish to withdraw, even if some way of escape were open. ... This mind restrains itself from sinning, not out of dread of punishment alone; but because it loves and reveres God as Father, it worships and adores him as Lord. Even if there were no hell, it would still shudder at offending him alone.[2]

Love, without a proper and holy fear of the Lord, soon degenerates into religious sentimentality. And the fear of the Lord devoid of holy love degenerates into dead orthodoxy. We cannot truly know the one without the other. And we do not truly know God until we know both.

The Fear of the Lord

Part of the reason we do not know the fear of God is that our notions about fear are mistaken. Fear isn't always a negative experience; at times we delight in it! That's why Stephen King is such a popular author and why the films *Jaws* or *The Exorcist* were hits. People line up to pay for being scared out of their wits.

When my children were younger they had a favorite game called "Lion." It was simple: we would shut off the lights after dark, and then, after counting to twenty-five, I would come roaring after them. I was the hungry Lion. The point was to catch them and eat them up. Between my roaring, their screaming and laughter, and the three of us thundering up and down several flights of stairs, the tension could reach a fever pitch. Potty breaks regularly halted the action. They loved the game, and often requested we play it. Even though they were afraid, if the tension got too great they'd suddenly turn and come running into my arms for comfort. Love coexisted easily with fear when we played Lion.

The Scriptures record several instances when individuals are ushered into the very presence of the Lord of Hosts (Is 6; Rev 1). They had no time to pause and reflect on what a proper response should be. Their response was instantaneous and complete. Falling on their faces, they were totally overwhelmed with an awful dread. "Woe to me!" Isaiah exclaimed. "I am ruined!"

Evangelicals commonly speak of knowing God personally. They sometimes claim to have a special "sense of his presence." Yet, seldom is there much evidence of the fear of the Lord. When we do speak of it, it is largely to explain it away: It doesn't mean real fear, just a proper reverence. Could it be that our lack of holy fear of the Lord is an indication that we do not know him as he is?

What we need, finally, is not a study of fear, but a clearer revelation of God. God's self-disclosure in Scripture gives us several ways in which we can come to grasp a proper fear of him. Here we'll touch on two: the nature of creation and the wrath of God.

Out of Nothing

Scientists tell us that the solid objects around us are actually not so solid as they appear. Viewed at the atomic level, even a piece of rock is primarily empty space. The space between subatomic particles is immense compared to the tiny particles themselves. Yet the rock seems solid and compact to us. But that is just a taste of creation's mystery and nature.

Part of the central teaching of the Judeo-Christian faith is that God created the universe out of nothing. By the power of his Word he called into being all that is. He did not, in pantheistic fashion, take part of his own being or essence and transform it into the universe. He spoke, and it was.

The Bible also teaches us that God continues to uphold his creation moment by moment, "sustaining all things by his powerful word" (Heb 1:3). What this means is that we, along with all of the creation, hang suspended over the nothing from which we were called. If God were to choose to withdraw his creative Word, we would instantly fall back into the absolute nothingness from which we came.[3] Moment by moment we are that close to the abyss. This is the true nature of creation. This we must not forget.

But our minds have been inoculated against such wonders. Seduced by the Enlightenment theory, wherein man's mind can comprehend and reduce nature to formulas, we lose sight of the wonder of God's creation. Meditate deeply on the nature of it. Read carefully the closing chapters of Job when he is confronted by the full majesty of God. Imagine God addressing these words to us:

> Brace yourself like a man;
>   I will question you,
>   and you shall answer me.
>
> Where were you when I laid the earth's foundation?
>   Tell me, if you understand.
> Who marked off its dimensions? . . .
>
> Have you ever given orders to the morning,
>   or shown the dawn its place?
>   (Job 38:3-4, 12)

If we think long and hard of what it might be like to be face to face with our Creator, we will begin to know a sliver of what it means to fear the Lord. When we know something of that, we will be energized for service with a holy love. When we realize that it is our Father that we're serving, we are forever humbled. But there's more to motivate us to a healthy, holy fear.

The Wrath of God

The Creator who called us out of nothing has revealed himself in history and Scripture as a God of wrath.[4] As Garrison Keillor points out: "In the Bible, people who innovated tended to get smote, and that at a time when God smote hard: when He smote you stayed smitten, smiting was no slap on the wrist."[5]

Keillor's assessment is correct. Think of Korah, Dathan and Abiram who rebelled against Moses' leadership (Num 16). God's reaction was unmistakable. The earth opened beneath their feet as they "were standing with their wives, children and little ones at the entrances to their tents" (v. 27). They fell into the chasm, and the nation heard their screams as the ground closed over them. That is the wrath of God.

Achan took a few small items out of the captured city of Jericho (Josh 7). God had said they were to take nothing; the entire place was devoted to himself. But Achan saw some gold, some silver coins and a robe. You could hardly blame him. It wasn't much, really, and they'd been stuck out in the desert for forty long years. Still, he did what was forbidden and judgment came. The people stoned him and his family to death, burning their bodies and heaping rocks up over their charred remains. "Then the LORD turned from his fierce anger" (v. 26).

The entire conquest of Canaan was a bloody affair and all at the Lord's command. So was the command to King Saul to destroy the Amalekites (1 Sam 15). The Lord's word is painfully explicit: "Now go, attack the Amalekites and totally destroy everything that belongs to them. Do not spare them; put to death men and women, children and infants, cattle and sheep, camels and donkeys" (v. 3).

But Saul was a bit more humane than that, keeping the king and some of the best animals alive. And so the prophet denounced him. As a result, the kingship was passed to another family line.

Elijah slaughtered four hundred fifty prophets of Baal on Mount Carmel (1 Kings 18). Both Isaiah and Habakkuk prophesy about the Lord's use of cruel and wicked armies to be instruments of his judgment. And the Mosaic law listed numerous capital offenses, including blasphemy (Lev 24:10-16), which incurred stoning as punishment and homosexual behavior (Lev 20:13), which merited death.

Explaining Away God's Wrath

The problem we face in all this is that God's wrath appears to us not as righteousness, but as harshness and cruelty. We feel not fear, but revulsion and a deep sense of injustice. How can God command and do such things? Is this the God we worship? Is this the God and Father of our Lord Jesus Christ?

One solution proffered is that this is the "God of the Old Testament" or "the Old Testament picture of God." Through Christ we have a more accurate or complete conception of his nature and actions. The New Testament God, the theory says, is a God of love. All of the above examples, which are from the Old Testament, compose a very primitive, almost barbaric face of God.

The problem is that this explanation doesn't fit the facts. The Old Testament is also full of grace (Jon 4:1-2; Ps 32), and the New Testament also speaks of God's wrath (Acts 5; 1 Cor 11:27-34; Heb 10:26-31; Rev 6—18). The Bible is unified in its revelation of God. The God and Father of our Lord Jesus is the God of Mount Sinai.

Another attempt to reconcile these two aspects of God is to drive a wedge between fact and faith, between mind and heart. *This doctrine is nothing to worry about,* we are told. *Just believe, don't think so hard. Flow with the Spirit and ignore theology.* After all, it's wrangling over dogma that has kept Christians divided over the centuries. When we come to Jesus we experience him as love, and that's all that matters—or so the theory goes.

But this too is contrary to the Word of God. We are commanded to love God with both mind and heart.[6] If we reject the witness of Scripture, we have no sure knowledge of God. The Bible insists upon itself as the trustworthy revelation of the Father. We spurn sound doctrine at our peril (1 Tim 1:10; 4:1, 6, 13, 16; 6:3).

Most evangelicals solve the dilemma of these passages on

God's wrath by a simpler method: Ignoring them. We emphasize the lighter side of God, with which we are more comfortable. We speak of his judgment in eternity, of course, but that's rather far removed. Instead, we spend most of our time in passages which reveal a God we can relax with.

This is wrong. We must know *God,* not some imaginary version of him filtered through our selective sensibilities. We can end up worshipping not the God who exists, but the image we have created in our imaginations. "You thought I was altogether like you," warns the God of Scripture. "But I will rebuke you" (Ps 50:21).

How then, shall we reconcile these difficult passages about the wrath of God? We must approach them as a faithful child would. We must say with Moses, "Now show me your glory" (Ex 33:18). But be warned: to know him is to know fear. And do not think that by "fear" I merely imply some sort of vague reverence. I mean *fear;* mere reverence is not enough to make a person fall down as "though dead" (Rev 1:17).

R. C. Sproul helps us understand the wrath of God by pointing out that we look at these passages from the wrong vantage point.[7] If we look at them from the perspective of Creation, then what do we see? In the Garden, every sin was a capital offense: "When you eat of [the tree of knowledge]," God warned them, "you will surely die" (Gen 2:17). Through his warning, we understand God's hatred of sin. "The wages of sin," Paul tells us, "is death" (Rom 6:23). It suddenly becomes clear that if sinners faced only justice at the hands of God, death would be the verdict. Our wickedness separates us from him. Because God's law and actions are pure and just, every sinner would die without exception if justice were the only measure.

But Adam and Eve didn't fall down dead. True, death came

crashing in on Creation with the Fall, but Adam and Eve still breathed by God's mercy. At Creation every sin was a capital offense; by the time of the Mosaic Law, God had reduced the number of capital offenses to a mere thirty or so. God's mercy is extended to his people despite the presence of sin.

We see God's mercy revealed in the account of the conquest of Canaan (Josh). God could have dealt with the Canaanites as he did the people of Noah's time, sparing only one family in the flood. Instead he extended grace to an entire nation. Israel received mercy, Canaan received justice—even though sin deserves death.

Uzzah's Problem

Few portions of Scripture reveal the problem of understanding God's wrath more clearly than Uzzah's story (2 Sam 6). The Philistines had captured the Ark of the Covenant, the holiest piece of furniture in the Tabernacle. Now the Israelites had come to bring it home. "When they came to the threshing floor of Nacon, Uzzah reached out and took hold of the ark of God, because the oxen stumbled. The LORD's anger burned against Uzzah because of his irreverent act; therefore God struck him down and he died there beside the ark of God" (vv. 6-7).

How could this be? A celebration of joy is suddenly interrupted by divine judgment. What did Uzzah do that was wrong? He only meant to help.

This passage makes us face some very difficult issues: First, do you see an "irreverent act" here? Most modern Christians don't. At least they don't see anything worthy of death. But this is God's Word. So if God sees an irreverent act, and we do not, who's probably correct?

Uzzah's gesture, though perhaps well meant, was an irreverent act. God had made it clear that the Ark was never to be touched, for it was above the Ark that God's glory dwelt. And it was never to be transported on an ox cart, but on the shoulders of the priests. There were rings on its sides, and poles made to fit in them, so it could be carried properly. They knew all of this, but hadn't bothered to obey. The Law had warned them that disobedience flirted with the wrath of God. It is presumptuous for creatures to treat the throne of God as merely a familiar national treasure.

Still, this seems harsh. *All right,* we think, *so they did it wrong.* But from what we can tell in the passage, Uzzah's act was spontaneous. As he walked along at the side of the cart, the oxen stumbled, and the cart lurched. There was perhaps the danger that the Ark would slide off and fall. What if it broke or was soiled? Perhaps Uzzah cared so deeply about Yahweh's reputation that he couldn't bear to have the Ark even touch the dust. So spontaneously Uzzah reached out to steady it. And for that he died? Our sense of justice is offended.

Yet even here our thinking is hopelessly perverted. It is not dirt which would defile the Ark; dirt is not in rebellion against God. Man is. God created the dirt and called it good. It is man who is separated from God by sin, not the earth.

And still we question death meted out for a *spontaneous* act. A premeditated sin, perhaps, but an impulsive one? Once again, our thinking is off the mark. Why do we think that spontaneous acts are more acceptable simply because they're uncontrived? I will tell you about my own spontaneous sin. A sin that, to my shame, I have had to confess more times than I care to admit.

I have a picture of what "the good life" consists of, and occasionally I enjoy it: A good novel, peace and quiet, an easy chair, a cup of tea. But in the midst of such pleasure, my child may thunder in to interrupt: "Read me a story." "Where's Mom?" "Play a game with me!" "He's being mean to me." "She won't share." "I'm bored, what can I do?" Far too often, I explode in selfish anger: "Can't you see I'm busy? Get out of here—and stay out."

A parent's anger can crush a child. More than once I've watched little eyes fill up with tears. They hadn't meant wrong and I knew better. Was my action spontaneous? Certainly. Was it sin? I am convinced it was. There is no doubt in my mind that we can sin spontaneously, and that the wages of sin is death.

The mystery is not that Uzzah died. The mystery is that I still live. Uzzah did not receive mercy, true. He received justice. The question isn't why Uzzah received justice, but why have I been spared? Only by God's mercy.

R. C. Sproul notes that we have turned things around rather badly. We receive mercy upon mercy; then slowly we begin to take grace for granted. Soon we expect it as our rightful due, and that which was given as a gift is demanded as a right. Finally, in an ultimate act of perverted logic, we perceive any act of God's justice as injustice.

Now these passages on the wrath of God look very different. The God and Father of our Lord Jesus Christ is a God of wrath. But instead of the wrath we so rightly deserve, we have received grace. May we repent that we have taken his mercy so lightly while we've scorned his judgment. As we meditate deeply on this, we will begin to understand the fear of the Lord. And that fear will motivate us to adoration and faithfulness.

The Love of Christ
As we've already seen, it's impossible to try to separate God's

love and his wrath into two categories. As we bow before him, allowing the Scriptures to reveal him to us, we are brought face to face with his great and tender grace even as we see his wrath. Love and fear are inseparable responses to knowing God.

At Calvary this is made clear. At the cross God's wrath was poured out, not on us who deserved it, but on Christ. There we see his love for us and the extent of his mercy. The One who knew no sin became sin and suffered its penalty on our behalf. Through the death of his Son, the Judge of all the earth became our Father and friend.

Yet like embers slowly cooling, love can grow cold. What was initially so wonderful can become common and barely noticed over time. Like the Ephesians of the first century, we forsake our first love (Rev 2:4). When the Lord rebuked the Ephesians for having lost their love, he urged them to stir up their memory in order to repent and restore their love for Christ (Rev 2:5). We too need to look at God more clearly, and by his grace, remember what it means to love him.[8]

What we are to remember is the truth. The truth of our sin and what we deserve. The truth of God's mercy and what we have received in place of justice. The truth of God's wrath and what Christ mercifully suffered for us. This is the truth of Calvary.

But does the power of the cross no longer move us? It is possible that we have become too familiar with it. I once sat in an audience as a speaker described in detail the physical and spiritual trauma of the cross. He went over the cruel flogging, the thorns and the agony of the slow, painful hanging Jesus endured while nailed to a rough, wooden beam. Then he detailed the spiritual dimensions of his suffering, the bitter humiliation he faced. How he set aside his glory and took our sin on himself when he had known only utter perfection. Finally, the hell of separation from the Father, as the alienation of the Fall was taken up into the Trinity. All of us in the audience reacted as if it were just one more academic enterprise, listening calmly and furiously scribbling notes.

Then he told us the story of a tiny kitten. It was full of painful details, for death had come only after much torture at the hands of cruel children. We were deeply moved, and as he stretched out the story, someone finally asked him to stop. The gore of it and the pain we felt were bothersome. Our hearts had gone out to a kitten, but had remained cold toward our Lord.

Has the cross been reduced to a mere object of academic interest? It is as though we are so accustomed to our precious gem that it seems to us just one more stone. With a loss of remembering comes a loss of love. Now I'm not suggesting that every mention of Calvary should throw us into paroxysms of sorrow. Nor is there anything wrong with a carefully researched account of Calvary, or with note-taking. I am asking only if we know—and are motivated by—the love of Christ.

The Source of Motivation

Thinking Christianly about success means we must be concerned about the driving force in our lives. What is our source of motivation? What stirs us to action, what moves our heart?

A zeal for pleasing the Lord witnesses to godly motivation. And the only adequate sources of motivation for pleasing God are the fear of the Lord and the love of Christ.

To know God is to know the fear of the Lord. It is to know something of the horror of sin and the awesome character of God's holiness. It is to wonder why we still live and Uzzah died. It is to be filled with a righteous jealousy and holy fervor for the glory of God.

To know God is to know the love of Christ. It is to be filled with a consuming passion for him. It is to know something of the depths of grace and the breathtaking character of God's mercy. It is to be filled with wonder that we who so richly deserve death still breathe.

Dr. Hans Rookmaaker was an art historian who was on fire with a passion for the truth of God. Throughout his life he was unflagging in his insistence that Jesus Christ was Lord. One time a student complained of being tired of fighting for the truth. It was so wearisome and so seemingly endless. Rookmaaker's reply was a measure of how well he knew the Lord. Here is the response of one whose passion was informed by the fear of the Lord and the love of Christ:

> You are tired! I am sorry for you! I am not tired yet. I have fought for the Bible for most of my life. . . . And now you are weeping! Never mind. Weep for the right things. Weep because the truth of God is being thrown away and what will our world do without it? Men will never find other moral standards that they will build society on, never doubt that. . . . You cannot imagine what it is like when men turn away from God. The thought should make you go cold. . . . I have fought for the truth of the Bible for thirty years. But are you tired already? How can you be? How do you dare?[9]

This is not harshness or legalism. It is a response born of supreme faithfulness, and reveals a heart and mind set upon God, righteously motivated to serve him.

Another godly servant was Betty Stam, who was in China with her husband around the turn of the century. Her desire was to live a life of faithfulness before the Lord. In her Bible was this prayer. It is a prayer of consecration, a prayer of faithfulness that reflects a passion born in one who knows the fear and love of God. It is a prayer we need to adopt for ourselves, yet only if we can honestly accept the cost of such devotion. The Stams were missionaries, and when revolution broke out in China, the Stams were beheaded.

> I give up all my own plans and purposes,
>   all my own desires and hopes,
>   and accept thy will for my life.
> I give myself, my life, my all
>   utterly to thee to be thine forever.
> Fill me with thy Holy Spirit,
>   use me as thou will,
>   send me where thou will,
>   work out thy whole will in my life
>   at any cost.
> Now and forever. Amen.

The Only True Success

The Lord has promised to return, and when he does there will be an accounting. All those who serve his cause are known by him, for he is a personal God. As stewards we will be required to explain how we have used his good gifts. Our choices and actions have been significant. What we have done is important, and on that day we will be able to report to the One who loved us enough to die for us.

There, before all the assembled hosts of cherubim and angels, before all the redeemed of the Lord, before all of created reality, each of us will be called by name. It will be our turn to step forward and present to the Lord the results of our faithfulness. As we do so, we will see him as he is, complete with the marks of Calvary.

The significance of our faithfulness—or lack of it—will be reflected as the Lord of lords comments on it specifically. The Scriptures tell us that there is the very real possibility that when we have finished our report, he will respond in praise. There remains the possibility that we will actually hear him say:

"Well done! Good job! I am pleased! You have been faithful!
Now come, enter into my home and my rest for
   all eternity!"

That is success.

Questions for Individuals and Groups

1. What motivations for life and success are common in your family background?

2. What motivates people in your church? To what extent are these motivations adequate for the Christian?

3. How can a better comprehension of the nature of creation help engender a healthier fear of God?

4. How can we grow in our appreciation for the God of nature?

5. How are you used to responding to the passages which reveal the wrath of God? Why?

6. Do you think we should fear God or not? Explain.

7. What factors in our backgrounds, our society and the church prevent us from fearing God the way we should?

8. In what ways have you, like the Ephesians of Revelation 2, lost your first love? What will you do now?

9. What hinders you from praying Betty Stam's prayer? What fears do you have?

10. How can we be better stewards now in light of the coming judgment?

The care that is filling your mind at this moment, or but waiting till you lay the book aside to leap upon you—that need which is no need, is a demon sucking at the spring of your life.

No, mine is a reasonable care—an unavoidable care, indeed.

Is it something you have to do this very moment?

No.

Then you are allowing it to usurp the place of something that is required of you this moment.

There is nothing required of me at this moment.

Nay, but there is—the greatest thing that can be required of man.

Pray, what is it?

Trust in the living God.

I do trust Him in spiritual matters.

Everything is an affair of the spirit.

George MacDonald

Notes

Opening Epigraph
[1] J. R. R. Tolkien, *The Fellowship of the Ring*, 2nd Rev. Ed. (London, Allen and Unwin, 1966), p. 231.

Chapter 1: Something Everyone Wants
[1] "Suicide: The Black Cloud," *InterVarsity* magazine, Winter 1984, p. 14.
[2] This is one implication of the biblical teaching concerning dominion in Gen 1—2. See chapter seven for more on this theme, as well as Ranald Macaulay and Jerram Barrs, *Christianity with a Human Face* (Leicester: Inter-Varsity Press, 1979) and Dick Keyes, *Beyond Identity* (Hodder and Stoughton, 1986).
[3] An interesting and eloquent analysis of this phenomenon from a non-Christian perspective is Allan Bloom, *The Closing of the American Mind* (New York: Simon and Schuster, 1987).
[4] Christopher Lasch, *The Culture of Narcissism: American Life in an Age of Diminishing Expectations* (London: Abacus Press, 1980), p. 47.
[5] This film is 95 minutes in length and was released in 1985. It was written and directed by John Hughes.

[6]Dr. Paul Rosch, president of the American Institute of Stress, quoted by Lawrence Maloney in "SUCCESS! The Chase Is Back in Style Again," *U.S. News and World Report*, Oct. 3, 1983, p. 60.

Chapter 2: Christian Views of Success
[1]Stephen D. Eyre, *Defeating the Dragons of the World* (Downers Grove, Ill.: InterVarsity Press, 1987), p. 27.

Chapter 3: The World's Measure of Success
[1]One film example is *Wall Street*, directed by Oliver Stone and starring Michael Douglas, Charlie Sheen and Daryl Hannah. A novel that strips away the shallowness of modern culture is Tom Wolfe, *The Bonfire of the Vanities* (London: Cape, 1988).
[2]Dinah Prince, "Why One Wonder Woman Packed It In," *New York*, July 15, 1985, pp. 42-47.
[3]Ibid., p. 43.
[4]Ibid.
[5]Ibid., p. 44
[6]Ibid.
[7]Ibid., pp. 46-47.
[8]For one example, see Richard West, "An American Family/Roots: The Mexican Version," *Texas Monthly*, March 1980, pp. 109-19, 166-81.
[9]See, for example, *The Concise Oxford Dictionary:* seventh edition (Oxford: Oxford University Press, 1982): "*Success* . . . attainment of wealth or fame or position . . ."; and Anthony Campolo, *The Success Fantasy* (Wheaton, Ill.: Victor Books, 1980)—"In our culture *success* means an individual has gained for himself one, if not all, of the following: wealth, power, and prestige" (p. 9).
[10]Carl Sagan, *Cosmos* (London: Macdonald Futura, 1981), p. 4.
[11]Francis Schaeffer, *How Should We Then Live?* (London: Hodder and Stoughton, 1976), p. 205.
[12]Lasch, *Culture of Narcissism*, p. 60.
[13]Daniel Yankelovich, *New Rules* (London: Abacus Press, 1980), p. xx.
[14]Ibid., p. 8.
[15]Ibid., p. 9.
[16]Ibid., p. 10.
[17]Lasch, *Culture of Narcissism*, p. 59.
[18]From an advertisement for Egon von Furstenberg's *The Power Look* (New York: Fawcett Book Group, 1979).

[19] Calvin Seerveld, *Rainbows for the Fallen World* (Toronto: Tuppence Press, 1980). See page 42ff.

[20] Malcolm Muggeridge, *Jesus Rediscovered*, quoted in *HIS* magazine, April 1973, p.3, and published by Fount Paperbacks, 1979.

Chapter 4: Where Success and Idolatry Meet

[1] Ingmar Bergman, *The Magic Lantern: An Autobiography* (New York: Viking, 1988), p. 204.

[2] Herbert Schlossberg, *Idols for Destruction* (Nashville, Tenn.: Thomas Nelson, 1983), p. 6.

[3] See Psalm 115:3-8, Romans 1:18-32 and 2 Corinthians 3:7-18.

[4] David Kipnis, "The View from the Top: Successful Uses of Power Corrupts How We See Those We Control," *Psychology Today*, December 1984, p. 30.

[5] Books that are helpful here include Os Guinness, *The Gravedigger File* (London: Hodder and Stoughton, 1983) and John White, *The Golden Cow* (Basingstoke: Lakeland, 1980).

[6] I owe this idea to "Ash Heap Lives," a sermon by Francis Schaeffer published in *No Little People* (Downers Grove, Ill.: InterVarsity Press, 1974).

[7] Maloney, "SUCCESS," p. 60.

[8] Charles Colson, "A Call to Rescue the Yuppies," *Christianity Today*, May 17, 1985, p. 20.

[9] Dorothy L. Sayers, "The Dogma Is the Drama," *The Whimsical Christian* (New York: MacMillan, 1978), p. 28.

[10] Schlossberg, *Idols for Destruction*, pp. 334-35.

Chapter 5: Case Studies in the Failure of Success

[1] This story appeared in *Eternity*, January 1969, p. 18.

[2] Carl Sagan, *Cosmos* (London: Macdonald Futura, 1981), p. 183n.

[3] See, for example, the statistics concerning this in George Gilder's *Men and Marriage*, rev. ed. (Gretna, Louis.: Pelican, 1986), pp. 51-59.

[4] Yankelovich, *New Rules*, p. 104.

[5] Merrill F. Unger, *Unger's Bible Dictionary* (Chicago: Moody Press, 1966), p. 570.

[6] D. Martyn Lloyd-Jones emphasizes this wonderfully in the sermons collected in *Revival* (Basingstoke: Marshall Pickering, 1988).

[7] Paul Johnson, *A History of the Jews* (London: Weidenfeld and Nicolson, 1987), p. 59.

[8] I am indebted for these historical details to *Unger's Bible Dictionary*.

Chapter 6: How God Uses the World's Success

[1] The historical data here was taken from *Unger's Bible Dictionary*, pp. 1094-96.

[2] Leland Ryken, *Worldly Saints* (Grand Rapids, Mich.: Zondervan, 1986), p.32.

[3] Charles Colson, "William Wilberforce" in *Chosen Vessels*, ed. Charles Turner (Ann Arbor, Mich.: Servant Publications, 1985), pp. 40-70.

[4] For further study: on a general critique of Western society from a biblical perspective see Schlossberg, *Idols for Destruction;* on a biblical view of economics see Brian Griffiths, *The Creation of Wealth* (London: Hodder and Stoughton, 1984) and Ronald Nash, *Poverty and Wealth* (Westchester, Ill.: Crossway Books, 1986); on a discussion of justice see Ronald Nash, *Social Justice and the Christian Church* (Milford, Mich.: Mott Media, 1983). Though it is written from a Thomistic perspective, Michael Novak, *The Spirit of Democratic Capitalism* (New York: Simon and Schuster, 1982), has some helpful analysis. For an in-depth treatment of the West's wealth and the Third World, see P. T. Bauer, *Equality, the Third World, and Economic Delusion* (Cambridge, Mass.: Harvard University Press, 1981).

[5] Jim Wallis, "The Powerful and the Powerless" in *Piety and Politics: Evangelicals and Fundamentalists Confront the World*, ed. Richard John Neuhaus and Michael Cromartie (Washington, D. C.: Ethics and Public Policy Center, Inc., 1987), p. 192.

[6] See, for example, Schlossberg, *Idols for Destruction;* and Marvin Olasky, "Unholy Alliance," *Eternity*, June 1985, pp. 19-23, and "Listen Hard, E. F. Hutton," *Eternity*, September 1985, p. 14.

[7] For a further discussion of this issue see Herbert Schlossberg, "Ideas, Gizmos, and Libertarian Power Brokers," *Eternity*, December 1986, pp. 29-32.

[8] Brian Griffiths, *Morality and the Market Place* (London: Hodder and Stoughton, 1982), p. 130.

[9] Brian Griffiths, *The Creation of Wealth* (London: Hodder and Stoughton, 1984), p. 14.

[10] Please do not misunderstand this term. By "creation of wealth" I am not referring to amassing affluence in a lifestyle of luxury. I am using it in a technical sense, referring to the increased value creativity and hard work bring when applied to God's creation.

[11] Griffiths, *Creation of Wealth*, p. 116.

[12]Arthur Pierson, *George Muller of Bristol* (Old Tappan, N. J.: Fleming H. Revell, 1899).

[13]See Charles Durham, *Temptation* (Downers Grove, Ill.: InterVarsity Press, 1982).

[14]"A Hymne to God the Father," in *Donne: Poetical Works*, ed. Herbert Grierson (Oxford: Oxford University Press, 1933), pp. 337-38.

[15]Charles Colson, "The Most Fearsome Judgment," *Christianity Today*, August 6, 1982, pp. 20-21.

[16]Ibid., p. 21.

[17]Ibid.

[18]Aleksandr Solzhenitsyn, "A World Split Apart," *National Review*, July 7, 1978, p. 839.

Chapter 7: Seeing Our Work the Way God Does

[1]Contributors to this article are: Kent Black, Duncan Christy, Louise Farr (Los Angeles), James Fallon (London), Mark Ganem and Christina Lynch (Milan), Leslie George (Paris), Joanna Ramsey (Washington), "Dream Jobs," *M: The Civilized Man*, March 1988, pp. 77-95.

[2]Ingmar Bergman, "The Snakeskin," *Persona and Shame: Two Screenplays* (London: Calder and Boyars Publishers, 1972), pp. 12-13.

[3]For an excellent study of the New Age, see Douglas Groothuis, *Unmasking the New Age* (Downers Grove, Ill.: InterVarsity Press, 1986).

[4]M. Scott Peck, *The Road Less Traveled: A New Psychology of Love, Traditional Values and Spiritual Growth* (London: Hutchinson, 1983), pp. 15-16.

[5]See, for example, Calvin *Institutes of the Christian Religion*, 1536 Edition 3.10.6.

[6]Quoted in Leland Ryken, *Worldly Saints: The Puritans As They Really Were* (Grand Rapids, Mich.: Zondervan Publishing House, 1986), p. 37.

[7]Gen 1:10, 12, 18, 21, 25, 31.

[8]Ranald Macaulay and Jerram Barrs, *Christianity with a Human Face* (Leicester: Inter-Varsity Press, 1979), pp. 9-10.

[9]See, for example, the New American Standard Bible translation of this verse.

[10]Bruce Milne, *Know the Truth: A Handbook of Christian Belief* (Leicester: Inter-Varsity Press, 1982), pp. 73-74.

[11]For further study see Macaulay and Barrs, *Christianity with a Human Face.*

[12]Quoted in Ryken, *Worldly Saints*, p.25.

[13]Quoted in Ryken, *Worldly Saints*, pp. 15, 25.

[14]I am indebted to Os Guinness's lectures and conversations with him for

much of my thinking about callings.

[15]Donald G. Bloesch, "Enthusiasm," *Faith and Its Counterfeits* (Downers Grove, Ill.: InterVarsity Press, 1981), pp. 61-72.

[16]See John R. W. Stott, *The Cross of Christ* (Leicester: Inter-Varsity Press, 1986), especially pp. 25-32.

[17]These include Jeremiah (Jeremiah 1); Moses (Exodus 3—6); Abraham (Genesis 12); Joseph (Genesis 37—47); and Paul (Acts 9).

[18]Quoted in Ryken, *Worldly Saints,* p.30.

[19]The Puritan Richard Baxter as quoted in Ryken, *Worldly Saints,* p. 58.

[20]James Sire, *The Universe Next Door* (Leicester: Inter-Varsity Press, second edition, 1988), flyleaf.

[21]John Milton, *Paradise Lost,* Book IX, in *An Introduction to Literature: Poetry,* ed. E. Volpe and M. Magalaner (New York: Random House, 1967), p. 88.

[22]For further study of why a rejection of the truth produces unhealthy polar extremes, see Herman Dooyeweerd, *Roots of Western Culture: Pagan, Secular, and Christian Options* (Pittsburgh, Penn.: Radix Books, 1979).

[23]I am indebted to an unpublished message by Steve Garber for this application of John 11.

Chapter 8: Faithfulness in Some Trouble Spots

[1]Taken from M. Á. Smith, *From Christ to Constantine* (London: Inter-Varsity Press, 1971), pp 86-91.

[2]"Work and Rest," p. 13, an unpublished paper by Paul Marshall of the Institute for Christian Studies in Toronto. Presented in March 1985 at Wheaton College at a conference entitled "Christian Theology in a Post-Christian World."

[3]"Persistence Is Key to Woman Broker's Success," *Chicago Tribune* (August 17, 1985).

[4]Marshall, "Work and Rest," p. 13.

[5]Ibid., p. 13.

[6]Ibid., pp. 13-14.

[7]See, for example, the delightful chapter "Sundays" in Laura Ingalls Wilder's *Little House in the Big Woods* (New York: Harper & Row, 1932), pp. 83-100. Sometimes the scope of rest is conceived of too narrowly. (See, for example, *The Westminster Confession,* The Larger Catechism, questions 115-21.) Because it is beyond the scope of this book, I do not fully treat the subject of the Sabbath's being observed by all of God's people.

[8] Frank Vanden Berg, *Abraham Kuyper: A Biography* (St. Catharines, Ontario: Paideia Press, 1978), p. 80.

[9] For practical guidance see Gordon MacDonald, *Ordering Your Private World* (Crowborough: Highland Books, 1987).

[10] See Charles Colson, *Loving God* (Grand Rapids, Mich.: Zondervan, 1983); J. I. Packer, *Knowing God* (London: Hodder and Stoughton, 1975); and Francis A. Schaeffer, *True Spirituality* (London: Hodder and Stoughton, 1972).

[11] For further study see John R. W. Stott, *Your Mind Matters* (London: Inter-Varsity Press, 1972); Harry Blamires, *The Christian Mind* (London: SPCK, 1963); and James W. Sire, *How to Read Slowly*, rev. ed. (Wheaton, Ill.: Harold Shaw, 1988).

[12] Os Guinness in a series of lectures given in October 1978 entitled "The Seductive Seventies."

[13] John White, *People in Prayer* (Leicester: Inter-Varsity Press, 1978), p. 16.

[14] Ibid., p. 17.

[15] This story is recorded as "Sam Brown's Ride" by Merle Potter in *101 Best Stories of Minnesota* (Minneapolis: Harrison and Smith, 1931), pp. 96-99.

[16] Ibid., p. 97.

[17] Ibid., p. 99.

[18] See Mt 26:14—27:10; Mk 14:10-26, 43-50; Lk 22:1-53; Acts 1:16-25.

[19] See Lis Harris, *Holy Days: The World of a Hassidic Family* (New York, N.Y.: Summit Books, 1985) for a delightful introduction to Passover observance in modern Jewish families.

[20] See Mt 26:31-75; Mk 14:27-52, 66-72; 16:1-8; Lk 22:7-62; 24:1-12.

[21] Bruce Milne, *Know the Truth* (Leicester: Inter-Varsity Press, 1982), p. 103.

[22] For further study see John R. W. Stott, *Basic Christianity* (London: Inter-Varsity Press, second edition, 1971); Leon Morris, *The Atonement* (Leicester: Inter-Varsity Press, 1983); and John R. W. Stott, *The Cross of Christ* (Leicester: Inter-Varsity Press, 1986).

[23] Dick Keyes, "The Meaning of Shame and Guilt," *What in the World Is Real?* (Champaign, Ill.: Communication Institute, 1982), p. 104.

[24] Ibid., p. 103.

[25] For further study see Dick Keyes, *Beyond Identity* (London: Hodder and Stoughton, 1986).

[26] See Charles Colson, *Loving God* (Grand Rapids, Mich.: Zondervan, 1983); and John White and Ken Blue, *Healing the Wounded: The Costly Love of Church Discipline* (Leicester: Inter-Varsity Press, 1985).

[27] Keyes, *Beyond Identity*, p. 105.

Chapter 9: What the World Didn't Tell You about Motivation

[1] See, for example, 2 Corinthians 5:11, 14.

[2] John Calvin, *Institutes of the Christian Religion* (Philadelphia, Penn.: Westminster, 1960), pp. 42-43.

[3] Milne, *Know the Truth*, pp. 72-74.

[4] I am deeply indebted to J. I. Packer's *Knowing God* (London: Hodder and Stoughton, 1975) and R. C. Sproul's taped series of messages "The Holiness of God" for my thinking about the wrath of God. Their ministry to me in this area is so foundational that this section of the book should be properly thought of as co-authored by them.

[5] Garrison Keillor, *Lake Wobegon Days* (London: Faber, 1986), p. 136n.

[6] See Stott, *Your Mind Matters*, and Packer, *Knowing God*, especially chapter one, "The Study of God."

[7] See R. C. Sproul, *The Holiness of God* (Wheaton, Ill.: Tyndale, 1985).

[8] A helpful book on this topic is Os Guinness, *Doubt* (Tring: Lion, 1983).

[9] Linette Martin, *Hans Rookmaaker* (London: Hodder and Stoughton, 1979), pp. 140-41.

Laid-back Religion?
A penetrating look at Christianity today

J. I. PACKER

Have contemporary Christians diluted the faith and wrapped themselves in layers of material comfort?

This is just one of the pertinent questions asked, and answered, by J. I. Packer in this fresh scrutiny of the state of the faith today.

With his usual wisdom and wit, he stimulates us to reflect on what it means to be a Christian at the end of the twentieth century. Here we have 'vintage Packer' calling us to God-centred holiness (which brings true joy) amid our culture's frantic pleasure-seeking.

160 pages   *B format*

Inter-Varsity Press

Desiring God
JOHN PIPER

"This is a serious book about being happy in God." We find our deepest, most enduring happiness only in him – the God in whom Scripture commands us to rejoice.

This God-centred joy, writes John Piper, is fuelled by worship, prayer and the Bible, and spills over to others in service and mission. As we practice this "Christian hedonism", we shall realize our destiny – "to glorify God by enjoying him forever".

"The healthy biblical realism of this study in Christian motivation comes as a breath of fresh air."

J. I. Packer

John Piper is senior pastor at Bethlehem Baptist Church in Minneapolis.

288 pages   *B format*

Inter-Varsity Press

The Time of Your Life
ALAN MACDONALD,
TONY CAMPOLO and others

If you've wondered whether parties and drinking, sport, films or social action are the best use of your time, then read this lively and fast-moving guide. It looks at how to make the most of time – with friends, enjoying yourself and helping others.

Alan MacDonald is a freelance writer and former director of Footprints Theatre Company. Tony Campolo is an American professor who has been a main speaker at Greenbelt.

96 pages   *Large paperback*

Frameworks

Eros Defiled
JOHN WHITE

To be human is to be sexual. That's the way God made us.

Yet many people – Christians included – are tormented by their sexuality. The problem may be frustration, masturbation, premarital sex and perhaps pregnancy, an 'affair', homosexuality, or strange compulsions.

To those people and their counsellors, John White offers compassion, help and hope.

'... a refreshing direct book. It ... shows a great deal of sensitivity, and has no fear of straight speaking.' *Christian Weekly Newspapers*

'The book's arguments are carefully anchored in the Bible. Undoubtedly *Eros Defiled* should be required reading for all in the pastoral ministry ... Youth leaders ... parents too. It can be recommended also to Christian adolescents in their late teens.'

Evangelical Times

168 pages   Pocketbook

Inter-Varsity Press

The Cost of Commitment
JOHN WHITE

'For years I felt guilty because I never seemed to be committed deeply enough to Christ ... I had the feeling that I should be suffering more, doing without more. Yet when I did suffer, my suffering bore little relationship to my commitment. Sometimes it seemed to arise from my lack of commitment and at other times bore no relation at all to it ...

'When Jesus tells you to take up your cross daily, he is not telling you to find some way to suffering daily. He is simply giving forewarning of what happens to the person who follows him.'

A warm and personal book to help Christians count the cost of commitment.

'... message is presented in a lucid, readable, at times very moving style ...' *Evangelical Times*

'... useful book to place into the hands of those who have recently made the great decision.' *Christian Herald*

92 pages   Pocketbook

Inter-Varsity Press

Too Busy Not To Pray
Slowing down to be with God
BILL HYBELS

"For many years", confesses Bill Hybels, "I knew more about prayer than I ever practised."

Does that sound familiar? Most of us feel a niggling guilt at not 'praying enough'. Prayer takes time and stillness – and we're so **busy**!

Bill Hybels found a way out, "I did something absolutely radical," he says, "I prayed."

Now he shares what prompted him to take that life-changing step, and how you too can embark on the same adventure.

Bill Hybels is Senior Pastor of Willow Creek Community Church, South Barrington, Illinois.

160 pages   Pocketbook

Inter-Varsity Press